Awakening
A Soul Whisperer's Guide to Remembering

Book One of Seven

The Soul Whisperer Series

JaiViibes

Awakening: A Soul Whisperer's Guide to Remembering
Book One of Seven in The Soul Whisperer Series

Copyright © 2025 Lliaily LLC. All rights reserved.

No part of this publication may be reproduced, stored in a retrieval system, or transmitted in any form or by any means—electronic, mechanical, photocopying, recording, or otherwise—without prior written permission from the author, except in the case of brief quotations used in reviews, articles, or scholarly works as permitted under United States copyright law.

Published by Soul Whisperer Press
Sheridan, Wyoming USA
An imprint of Lliaily LLC

Library of Congress Control Number: 2025947391

ISBNs
978-1-969525-00-1 (paperback)
978-1-969525-01-8 (eBook)

Cover design by JaiViibes™
Interior design by JaiViibes™

Disclaimer:
This book is intended for informational and inspirational purposes only and is not a substitute for professional medical, psychological, legal, or financial advice. The author does not offer or prescribe any treatment for physical, emotional, or mental conditions. Always consult a licensed professional before beginning any practice or approach discussed herein.

The information shared reflects personal insights and is offered as personal perspective. Use of this material is voluntary and at your own discretion. The author and publisher disclaim any liability for outcomes resulting from its use.

Dedication

To the Journey, and Those Who Walk Beside Us

To the pain that cracked us open,
and the grace that poured through the wound.
To the moments we thought we wouldn't make it—
and somehow, still rose.
To the darkness that carved space for light,
and to the ache that became our compass home.

To the Wisdom Keepers, who remember.
To the Medicine Carriers, who offer
their hands and hearts.
To the Song Collectors,
who preserve the soul's music.
To the Connectors, who weave the invisible threads.
To the Faith Keepers,
who believe when belief is hard.
To the Helpers, the Supporters, and the Healers—
your presence is a balm to the world.

And to you, reader—
thank you for choosing to turn toward yourself.
Toward truth. Toward wholeness.
This book is a mirror, but the courage is all yours.

With reverence for the mystery,
gratitude for the path, and deepest love for my
Eternal Muse, soul of my soul.

JaiViibes

Contents

Introduction Book One Awakening   1
Chapter One Awakening   9
What is Awakening?   10
    The Moment the Veil Lifts   13
    The Cracking Seed   14
    The Kingdom Within   15
    The Wave and The Ocean   16
    The Sculptor Beneath the Stone   17
    A Quiet Morning in Brooklyn   18
    The Shattering a Modern Initiation   19
    The Invitation   20
Chapter Two Why Awakening Hurts   23
Pain Becomes Portal   24
    The Death of Illusion   25
    The Ego's Grief   26
    The Loneliness of Seeing Clearly   26
    When the Heart Breaks Open   28
    The Pain of Disidentification   29
    Suffering as Sacred Alchemy   30
    The Hidden Gift in the Hurt   31
Chapter Three The Fivefold Human The Trinity & Something Real   33
The Mirage of Perception   34
The Trinity of Soul, Self, and Creation [see appendix A & B]   36
The Fivefold Map of Embodied Awakening   41
    The Body: The Temple of Form *Archetypal Orientation*   42
    The Body's Map   43
    Bringing the Body Online   44
    The Mind: The Architect of Perception   45
    The Mind's Map   46
    Bringing the Mind Online   47
    Heart: The Seat of Coherence   48

The Heart's Map	49
Bringing the Heart Online	50
Intuition: The Bridge Between Worlds	51
The Intuition's Map	52
Bringing Intuition Online	53
Soul: The Eternal Spark	54
The Soul's Map	55
Bringing the Soul Online	56
Bringing The Five Online	58
Alignment — When All Bodies Sing	59
Alignment Map	60
Bringing Alignment Online	61
Feeling, Emotion, and Inner Atmospheres	63
The Return to the Real	64

Chapter Four The Dark Night of the Soul 69

The Dark Night as the Realization of Disconnection	70
The Collapse of False Identity	73
The Absence of Light as Grace	75
Spiritual Despair as Sacred Ground	77
Detachment as Initiation	79
The Ego's Surrender	82
The Self Realigns as the Soul Emerges	84
Unknowing as Transformation	86
Feeling Forsaken: The Christ Parallel	88
The Alchemy of Suffering	90
From Darkness to Devotion	91
The Threshold of Integration	94

Chapter Five Deeper Exploration of Awakening 100

Introduction	101
Physical Awakening *Body - Nervous System - Survival Awareness*	103
The Body: Portal of Awakening	103
The Body as Portal	104
The Nervous System: Keeper of Memory	104
Signals of Physical Awakening	105

- The Shadow of Disembodiment — 105
- Dimensions of Awakening: BODY - The Gate of Sensation and Survival — 106

Mental Awakening *Mind - Belief Systems - Thought Awareness* — 110
- The Thought Matrix — 111
- The Inner Narrator: Deconstructing the Voice — 112
- Signs of Mental Awakening — 112
- The Shadow of Mental Awakening — 113
- Dimensions of Awakening: MIND - The Architect of Meaning and Belief — 114

Emotional Awakening *Heart - Feeling - Emotional Literacy* — 118
- The Intelligence of Feeling — 118
- The Breaking Open — 119
- Signs of Emotional Awakening — 121
- The Shadow of Emotional Awakening — 121
- Dimensions of Awakening: HEART – The Chamber of Longing and Recognition — 122

Intuitive Awakening *Subtle Knowing - Inner Guidance Nonlinear Insight* — 126
- The Language Beneath Thought — 126
- The Reclamation of Inner Guidance — 127
- Signs of Intuitive Awakening — 128
- The Shadow of Intuition — 128
- Dimensions of Awakening: INTUITION - The Compass of the Unspoken — 129

Soul Awakening *Presence - Essence - Divine Remembering* — 133
- The Essence Beneath the Story — 134
- The Great Unveiling — 134
- Signs of Soul Awakening — 135
- The Shadow of Soul Awakening — 135
- Dimensions of Awakening: SOUL - The Flame Behind All Seeing — 136

Closing Summary Book One: Awakening — 142

Appendix — 143

Introduction
Book One Awakening

The awakening process is often described as a deeply personal and transformative experience—an inner stirring that pulls us beyond the surface of life and into the mysteries of the soul. It is a call that cannot be ignored once heard, an invitation to dissolve the illusion of separation and remember the deeper essence of who and what we truly are.

Though unique to each individual, awakening tends to follow certain archetypal patterns. It begins with a disruption—a moment when the life we've built no longer feels real, fulfilling, or aligned. What once brought comfort begins to feel hollow. What once felt certain begins to unravel.

For me, it began with loss.

Not just the loss of relationships or opportunities, but the disintegration of the very scaffolding on which I had built my identity: career, reputation, material possessions, and the social structures that once defined my sense of self. One by one, they slipped away, like sand through grasping fingers. What was left was a profound silence—a void that both terrified and beckoned me.

In the solitude of that collapse, I found myself standing alone, staring at the sky, fists clenched, heart fractured, and spirit raw. I demanded answers—not from society, not from another person, but from something greater. I wanted truth—not the filtered, packaged truths of culture or religion—but something ancient, something real, something that could not be taken away.

What followed was not a single revelation, but a long, winding road paved with questions and stripped of guarantees. It was a soul pilgrimage. I devoured thousands of pages of spiritual teachings, sacred texts, psychology books, esoteric writings, and mystical poetry. I sat in stillness for ten days at a time in silent Vipassana meditation, peeling back layers of the mind. I trained in hypnotherapy and studied the subconscious terrain of trauma and belief. I journeyed with plant medicines in sacred ceremony, encountering archetypes, guides, and truths beyond language. I wept in therapy. I laughed in epiphanies. I raged at the sky, only to fall again into the arms of grace.

And slowly, something began to shift. The fog lifted. My senses sharpened. Old stories crumbled, and with them, the armor around my heart. In the space that opened, something long forgotten returned: a subtle but unmistakable connection to Spirit, to intuition, to knowing. What I had once dismissed as imagination revealed itself to be memory—ancestral, cosmic, soul-born memory. Gifts I had unknowingly suppressed began to reawaken. Visions. Messages. Synchronicities. A felt-sense of energy. The ability to feel beyond the physical.

The Soul Whisperer Series is the fruit of that journey. This is Book One in the series titled, *Awakening: A Soul Whisperer's Guide to Remembering*. This series is not a conclusion, but a living record of the path as it continues to unfold. It is written not as a manual, but as a mirror—a guide to support your own unique awakening, wherever you may be along the way. Through reflections, practices, soul inquiries, and spiritual truths gathered from experience and direct revelation, this book is here to remind you: you are not alone.

What is Awakening?

Awakening is not a spiritual high or momentary bliss. It is not an escape from life—it is a fuller entry into it. Awakening is the shedding of illusions, the stripping away of roles and rules that no longer serve, and the courageous act of facing what is real. It begins, often, in pain or confusion—but it ends in remembrance.

To awaken is to shift from the reactive mind to the receptive heart. It is to realize that we are not separate beings clawing for survival, but radiant expressions of a unified source, each of us playing our part in a grand unfolding.

Awakening is the process of seeing with clear eyes, loving with an open heart, and living in alignment with the soul's deepest truth. It is both a breakdown and a breakthrough. A death and a birth. A falling away and a coming home.

The Purpose of This Journey

The Soul Whisperer Series books one thru seven is not just a reflection of one person's path—it is a field of resonance. Whether you are in the tender beginning stages, navigating the intensity of transformation, or finding your footing in a new paradigm of consciousness, this book is here to walk with you. It offers not answers, but keys. Not doctrines, but doorways.

Let this be your invitation to remember. To trust your process. To hold space for your becoming. And to know that everything you are seeking is already within you, waiting to be revealed.

This is not a journey to some far-off enlightenment. It is a journey inward—to the truth, the wholeness, and the sacred intelligence of your own awakening soul.

Chapter One
Awakening

"Awakening arrives not by effort, but by grace—spontaneous and unbidden. It slips through the cracks when you're seeking, and sometimes even more when you've stopped. It is not a prize to be earned, but a terrifying gift—one that shatters illusions to reveal the truth beneath. You cannot force it, and yet it finds you the moment your soul becomes ripe for remembering."

What is Awakening?

"The eye through which I see God is the same eye through which God sees me."— *Meister Eckhart*

Awakening is not a moment—it is a movement of the soul. It is the subtle yet seismic shift when the inner world begins to outshine the outer one. No longer satisfied with inherited beliefs or borrowed dreams, something inside us stirs—a question, a longing, a whisper. We begin to feel, perhaps for the first time, that there is something more than this life we've been conditioned to live.

It is not the gaining of knowledge, but the remembering of truth. Awakening is the soul's quiet rebellion against the slumber of conformity. It's the sacred discontent that rises when the masks of identity begin to crack. We start to hear the echo of our own essence, calling us home through the static of the world. A new perception dawns—not as a blinding light, but as a slow turning toward the light within.

To awaken is to realize that the thoughts you think are not the totality of who you are. It is the disentangling from the story, the stepping back from the constant inner narration, and seeing—perhaps for the first time—that the narrator is not the one living your life. There is something deeper. Something still. Something eternal.

It is not always gentle. Sometimes awakening arrives as a storm. A breakup. A breakdown. A death. A moment where everything you've built shatters, not to destroy you, but to reveal you.

These initiations break the shell of illusion we mistook for reality. They do not come to punish, but to peel away. Like the cracking of a seed, they are violent only to the ego—but merciful to the soul.

Awakening is the shift from seeking to seeing.

> *"Stop searching. Let go of seeking and the truth will find you, not as something new, but as something always there, waiting to be seen."— Adyashanti*

But here, too, lies a paradox worth pausing for. Because before we see—we seek. Before we remember—we reach.

And yet, what if the seeking itself was already a sign that something in us had stirred?

There is a longing within us—a yearning, a holy ache—that compels us to move toward something we cannot quite name. We call it *seeking*. It is the hunger that leads us to teachers, to scriptures, to silence. To breakdowns, to mountaintops, to books that fall off shelves and moments that stop time.

And yet, as we walk the path, something becomes clear: Some awaken in a single breath. Others over years of shedding and becoming. Some feel it crash in like thunder. Others, like a slow dissolving mist. We imagine we are the ones climbing the mountain to find the truth. But perhaps the truth has been descending into us the entire time. They are not opposites. They are not even separate. They are lovers in a cosmic dance—one calls, the other answers. One reaches, the other reveals.

The soul has impeccable timing. It lets us wander far enough to forget, and then places a whisper in our chest: *Come home.* And when we finally pause, exhausted or cracked open, that whisper becomes a doorway.

We realize then that the seeking was never about acquiring anything new. It was about remembering what had always been within us.

We no longer look outward for salvation—we turn inward for remembrance. We begin to glimpse the sacred in all things: the golden light streaming through a window, the stranger's eyes that remind us of home, the silence between thoughts where God sometimes speaks.

It is a movement from fear to love. From separation to oneness. From thinking you are a wave, to realizing you are the ocean remembering itself in form. It is the birth of a new self that has always existed—unseen, but not absent. It is a return to consciousness. To essence. To the unshakable truth that you are not broken, not lost, not unworthy—but infinite, holy, and alive with light.

To awaken is to no longer live from reaction, but from revelation. It is not perfection. It is participation in the sacred unfolding of your true self.

You are not becoming someone different. You are unbecoming everything that is not you. Awakening does not add—it removes. Like Michelangelo seeing David in the marble, it chisels away the false until only truth remains.

It is not a destination, but a deepening. An ever-unfolding spiral inward, where each moment becomes an invitation to live more embodied, more heart, more soul. It is not a single experience, but a way of being—a remembering, again and again, that you are the light you have been searching for.

The Moment the Veil Lifts

"There comes a time when the seeking falls away, and in the silence that remains, truth reveals itself, not as something found, but as something that has always been."— Jack Kornfield

Awakening is a realization. A stripping away of everything that is not You. It is the quiet voice within that whispers: There is more than this.

In the world of schedules, stories, roles, and responsibilities, we become hypnotized by what is familiar. We wake each day and perform the identity we've inherited—believing we are the mask, the mood, the memory, the mistake. But awakening begins when we question the script.

When the patterns we've been living by lose their grip, and the life we've been building no longer feels like our own.

It may start as restlessness, as a quiet discomfort, or as a moment that shatters the ordinary—grief, love, synchronicity, or stillness. Something breaks open. Something ancient begins to stir. And the seeking begins.

Awakening is not about becoming someone new. It is about becoming real. It is a process of unlearning. It is the fog lifting from your inner landscape. You don't become someone else—you simply see yourself clearly, maybe for the first time.

It is the moment when the dream of who you thought you were begins to dissolve. Imagine this: You've lived your whole life inside a house with no windows. Everything you've ever known has been shaped within those walls. One day, a crack forms. Through that crack, light pours in. You see shadows dancing across the floor and realize—there is something beyond this house. That is awakening.

The Cracking Seed

The seed does not grow by adding more to itself. It grows by breaking open. What looks like destruction is often divine becoming.

> *"Sometimes, when you're in a dark place, you think you've been buried, but you've actually been planted."— Christine Caine*

The structures we cling to—the labels, the roles, the expectations—begin to crumble. Not out of cruelty, but because the soul cannot stay confined. The pain of awakening is not punishment. It is birth. The soil splitting to make way for roots. The shell cracking to reveal the life inside.

We are not broken when we awaken. We are simply no longer able to pretend.

The Kingdom Within

"The Kingdom is inside of you, and it is outside of you."
— *Gospel of Thomas*

Awakening reveals the sacred in everything—but especially in you. We are taught to seek divinity in far-off heavens, in doctrines, in distant futures. But the awakened eye sees the divine inward—in silence, in stillness, in self.

The kingdom is not a place. It is a presence. It is the space between thoughts. The peace beneath the chaos. The watcher behind the eyes. When you awaken, you stop searching for God in the sky and begin recognizing the holy in your own breath.

The Wave and The Ocean

Awakening is not the discovery of something new. It is the remembering of what has always been true.

> *"Enlightenment is when a wave realizes it is the ocean."*
> — *Thich Nhat Hanh (non-dual teaching)*

For so long, you believed you were just the wave—a name, a role, a story with a beginning and an end. You rose, you fell, you crashed against the shores of circumstance. But then something deeper pulls your awareness below the surface. You realize: I am not just the wave. I am the ocean expressing itself.

Not separate from Source, but sourced by it. Not apart from the Divine, but made of it. This is the holy recognition: You are not alone, not lost, not small. You are vast. Connected. Eternal. And you always were.

The Sculptor Beneath the Stone

"I saw the angel in the marble and carved until I set him free." — Michelangelo (paraphrased)

Awakening is not self-improvement. It is self-revelation. Awakening is not a process of adding more to yourself. It is the gentle, often painful process of letting go.

You are not here to become worthy. You are here to remember you already are. The masks. The roles. The identities you gathered for safety or survival. These are the stone. Your true nature—the Soul, the Essence, the Radiance—was always within. It only needed to be revealed.

Each experience that humbles you, softens you, or breaks your image of control is a chisel in the hands of the divine. It does not harm. It liberates. The sculptor is life. And the masterpiece… is who you've always been.

A Quiet Morning in Brooklyn

Julian was not the type you'd expect to awaken. A software architect with a condo in Brooklyn, a black coffee habit, and a schedule that left little space for mystery. He lived by logic, routine, and headphones. His inner world was organized into data, deadlines, and discreet distractions.

But something had been whispering— softly, at the edges of his sleep. One morning, power went out in the building. No internet. No coffee. No hum of machines. With nothing to do, Julian sat on the fire escape with a blanket and a cold mug of yesterday's tea.

For the first time in years, he watched the sky. Just… watched. A single leaf drifted down, spiraling slowly from a rooftop tree. And in that moment— without reason, instruction, or effort—something shifted.

The world didn't change. He did. It was as if the silence opened a door inside him. He felt himself being, rather than doing. He felt vast. Present. Still. Not as a thinker or achiever—but as awareness itself. There were no angels, no visions, no mantras. Just a leaf. And a breath. And the quiet realization: I am not my thoughts. I am the one who sees.

That morning became the hinge on which his life turned. Not outwardly—he still coded, still lived in the city. But inwardly, he never returned to sleep.

The Shattering a Modern Initiation

He did everything right. Husband. Father. Business owner. Provider. Protector. He followed the template with quiet pride—worked long hours, paid the bills, showed up for his family, carried the weight of being "the rock."

He believed in effort, in principle, in doing the right thing. He believed that if he honored the rules, the system would honor him. Then came the betrayal. An affair—not just a fracture in his marriage, but a fault line through his entire identity. His belief in love, in people, in order—shattered.

His motivation vanished. His trust in the social game disintegrated. Nothing made sense anymore. He was floating in a sea of disillusionment, unable to cling to the story of who he'd been. And one night, under a sky too silent to answer, he raised his fists and shouted:

"Bullshit. Show me something real."

It wasn't a prayer. It was a demand. No more roles. No more masks. No more pretending. That night, something ancient heard him and responded, not with words, but with felt awareness. And in that holy refusal to keep playing the false game, he crossed a threshold.

This was not the end. It was the beginning. The end of illusion, yes—but the beginning of Truth. The beginning of the real Game.

The Invitation

Awakening is not an answer. It is a doorway. You do not walk through it casually. The invitation does not come wrapped in light. It comes disguised—as heartbreak, as burnout, as a quiet ache for something you cannot name.

> *"The real voyage of discovery consists not in seeking new landscapes, but in having new eyes."* — *Marcel Proust*

This is your invitation. To stop pretending.
To stop performing. To stop negotiating
with the false.

You are not here to be perfect.
You are here to be real.
No more masks. No more mirrors.
You do not need fixing.
You need remembering.

Awakening begins the moment
you say "I am no longer willing
to sleep through my own life."
Yet for all its beauty, awakening
is not without its breaking.

The light we remember does not arrive without cost—it exposes what we must release. As the soul begins to rise, the self begins to crack. The very truths that set us free often first unravel us.

What was once familiar no longer fits. What once comforted now constrains. And so, begins the deeper initiation—not into bliss, but into becoming. This is where we turn next:

Into the ache beneath the awakening,
And the sacred pain that prepares the way.

And so, the light arrives—not as a comfort, not as warmth, but as fire. To awaken is to feel again. To see what we had numbed. To remember what we had buried. This is the moment where many turn back. Not because the path is false, but because it is true. And truth, when it first touches the tender places we've armored, does not soothe—it sears. Yes, the invitation is sacred. But stepping through it is an unraveling. Awakening opens the door, but it does not spare us the threshold. The light reveals, but it also burns. Before we rise, we break. And this—this is where the real journey begins. Into the hurt that heals. Into the pain that purifies.

Chapter Two
Why Awakening Hurts

*"The force that cracks the shell is the same force that
sets the soul free. Awakening reveals
who you've always been."*

Pain Becomes Portal

"Eventually you will see that the real cause of problems is not life itself. It's the commotion the mind makes about life that really causes the problems. Most of life will unfold in accordance with forces far outside your control... The moment in front of you is not bothering you. You are bothering yourself about the moment in front of you. It is not life's events but your reaction to them that is causing pain—and that pain can become a doorway to your freedom." — Michael A. Singer

Awakening is often imagined as an upward motion—into the light, into joy, into clarity. And eventually, it is. But first, it often feels like falling.

The descent comes before the rise.

For many, the moment of awakening is not serene but seismic. Not a gentle dawn, but a meteor striking the surface of your life, shattering everything in its blast radius. What once felt solid—your beliefs, your identity, your relationships—suddenly fractures under the intensity of newfound clarity.

To awaken is to see. But not just to see the beauty of truth. To awaken is to see the illusion fall apart. And that, dear soul, can hurt more than anything.

The Death of Illusion

The pain of awakening does not come from the truth. It comes from the loss of the lie.

We are not born into pure truth. We are born into systems—of thought, behavior, expectation. We inherit masks and call them identity. We are fed stories of success, of safety, of what it means to be good, or worthy, or lovable. And we believe them—because to belong, we must.

Until we begin to awaken.

And suddenly, we see. We see that the path we've walked was not ours. We see the invisible cages around our desires. We see how we traded authenticity for approval, and purpose for pretense.

The moment the illusion begins to die, there is panic. Our false scaffolding collapses. We grieve not because the illusion was real—but because we built our lives around it.

And when illusion dies, it doesn't die quietly. It dies screaming.

The Ego's Grief

> *"Your pain is the breaking of the shell that encloses your understanding."*—Kahlil Gibran

The ego is not evil—it is simply afraid. It is the part of you that believes it must protect you by maintaining control. It constructs your self-image, creates your plans, manages your reputation. And awakening is its undoing.

To the ego, awakening feels like death. It is.

But not death of the soul—death of the shell. Death of the actor. Death of the tightly held version of you that was never you to begin with.

And like any death, there is grief.

You may feel rage, despair, numbness, or disorientation. You may not recognize your reflection. You may wonder who you are, if you're losing your mind, or if you've ruined your life.

This is the grief of ego death. You are not dying. You are becoming real.

Grief is not failure. It is sacred mourning for the self that no longer fits. Let it come. Let it pass through you. For on the other side of grief is freedom.

The Loneliness of Seeing Clearly

There is a particular ache that comes when you begin to see what others do not.

You notice the unconsciousness in conversation, the posturing in social norms, the falsity in old friendships. You begin to crave depth, truth, stillness—and find that many around you are not ready to meet you there.

You try to speak what's awakening in you, and people look at you as though you've spoken a foreign tongue. You try to share your heart, and they redirect the topic back to the weather, or money, or surface-level news.

You feel like an outsider in your own life.

This loneliness is not a punishment. It is part of the passage. The old tribe cannot always walk with you through the threshold. But take heart: on the other side, new souls will recognize you. Your frequency will draw others who are also awakening. But first, there is the solitude of shedding. It is not the end of connection. It is the beginning of authenticity.

When the Heart Breaks Open

"The truth will set you free, but first it will make you miserable."
— James A. Garfield

The human heart is not made to remain closed. It wants to feel. It wants to love. It wants to expand. But years of hurt, fear, and numbing cause us to armor it.

Awakening rips the armor away.

And suddenly, you feel. Not just your own wounds, but the ache of the world. You feel beauty so deeply it hurts. You feel grief not just for your life, but for the collective pain of the planet. You feel the suffering of others as your own.

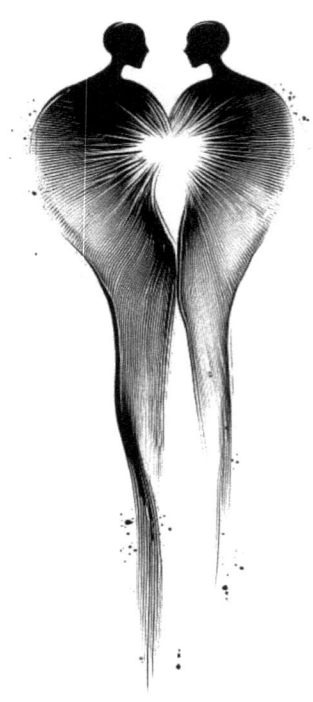

It can be overwhelming.
It can feel unbearable.

But this is not weakness.
This is divine sensitivity.

The heart is not breaking down.
It is breaking open.
To compassion.
To empathy.
To sacred vulnerability.

And from this center, your true strength begins to emerge.

The Pain of Disidentification

> *"It is no measure of health to be well adjusted to a profoundly sick society."* — Mark Vonnegut, The Eden Express (1975), often attributed to J. Krishnamurti.

You are not your name. Not your job. Not your trauma. Not your gender, ethnicity, religion, or resume.

But for most of your life, these were your anchors. You built your sense of self on these temporary labels. You mistook your story for your soul.

When awakening strips these away, it can feel like being skinned alive.

Who are you without your history? Who are you without your mask? Who are you without your role?

This identity loss is not annihilation—it is revelation.

It is the painful, beautiful, terrifying return to essence. To the eternal "I Am" that exists before any label, before any narrative. This shedding may feel like losing everything. But what you're losing was never the real you.

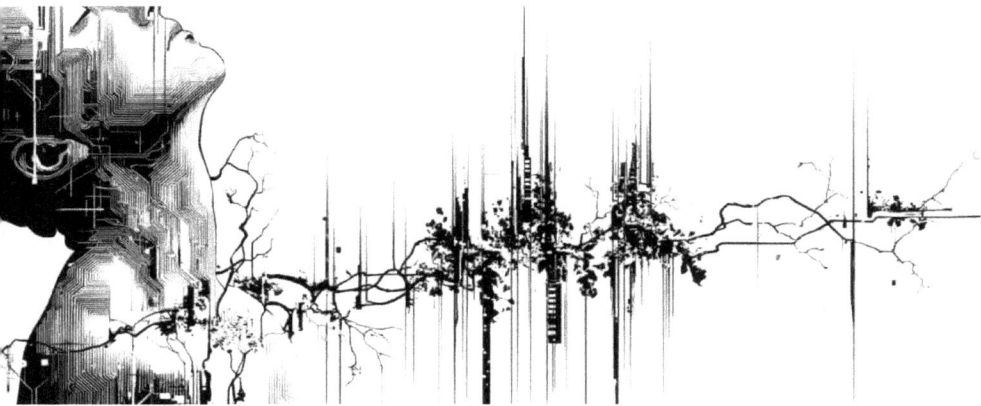

Suffering as Sacred Alchemy

> *"You do not heal 'from' trauma. You heal 'with' it."*
> — Resmaa Menakem

Pain is not always a punishment. In awakening, it is often a purifier.

Suffering is not always something to escape. Sometimes, it is a furnace where the soul is refined.

The same fire that burns away illusion also reveals truth. The same discomfort that makes you question everything also invites you to live in a new way.

The difference is how you meet it.

If you resist the pain, you prolong it. If you numb it, you miss its message. But if you meet as a feeling witness, if you let it burn what no longer serves, it becomes sacred.

This is suffering as alchemy.

It does not destroy you. It transfigures you.

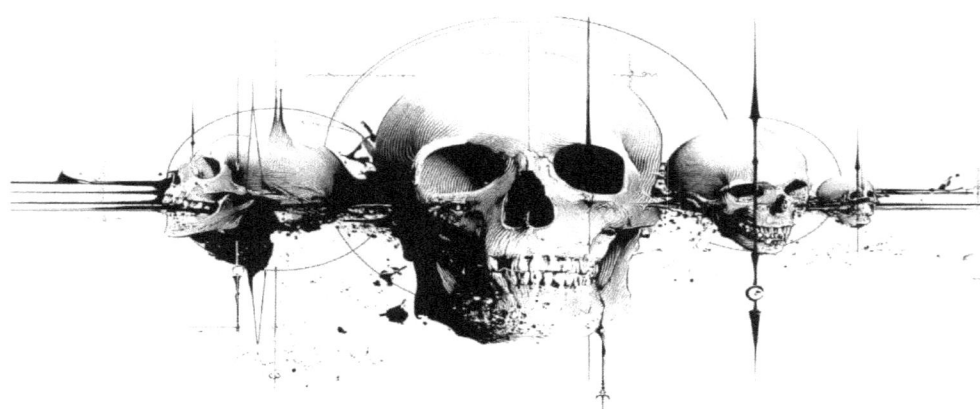

The Hidden Gift in the Hurt

Every soul who awakens will walk through fire.

But this fire is not here to consume you. It is here to reveal you.

What you lose, you never truly needed. What breaks you, also frees you. What hurts you, also heals you.

And in time, the wound becomes the womb. The pain becomes the portal. The sorrow becomes the song.

The gift of awakening is not just in what you gain—it is in what you release. And when the fire has passed, and the ashes settle, you will see: you were never the illusion. You were always the light beneath it.

The fire has done its work.
The illusions have fallen.
The ache has softened into silence.
And as the dust begins to settle,
a question stirs within:
If all that was false has
been stripped away…
what is real?
As we continue, we turn now
toward that quiet knowing—
not as something to seek,
but as something to recognize.
Chapter Three: Something Real.

Chapter Three
The Fivefold Human
The Trinity
& Something Real

*"There is a light in the soul that burns brighter than
any illusion, and when you touch it,
you remember what is real."*

The Mirage of Perception

The human experience unfolds through the lens of perception — shaped by thought, filtered through belief, colored by emotion, and projected onto a world we call "real." Yet ancient wisdom, particularly within the teachings of Buddhism, calls this world *maya* — not to suggest that nothing exists, but to remind us that what we see is not what is. *Maya* is the shimmering mirage on the horizon of the desert — beautiful, compelling, and entirely misleading. It is the dance of appearances: convincing, persistent, and ultimately impermanent.

We are born into a theater of forms — families, names, nationalities, genders, roles — and soon begin to equate these identities with reality itself. We learn early to measure our worth through success and our belonging through conformity. The world, as it is offered to us, becomes a complex play of projections. Our minds create meaning, stitch together stories, and install filters through which we interpret every experience. What we call reality is more often a feedback loop of conditioned perception — one in which we rarely question the script.

But beneath all this — beneath the accolades, the failures, the routines, and the rituals — there is a subtle pulse of dissonance. A quiet nudge that not everything we've been told is true. That perhaps what we've taken for substance is more akin to shadow play. The deeper truth is not absent — it is simply hidden behind the veil of form and familiarity.

To awaken is to pause long enough to feel the mirage. Not just to recognize it intellectually, but to experience its emptiness. To sit in the afterglow of success and still feel a void. To reach a long-sought destination and sense the absence of arrival. To lose what you thought mattered most and discover that you are still here.

> *"What we see is a reflection of our thoughts;*
> *what we feel is a reflection of our truth."*
> *— Ganga White*

These are cracks in the illusion — luminous fractures through which something eternal begins to shine.

Reality, as we have known it, is not solid. It is a living dream, woven by mind, shaped by memory, and held together by collective agreement. But truth is not destroyed by illusion. It is merely obscured. And if you listen closely — not with the ears, but with the soul — something begins to call from beneath the mirage.

There is something real. Not outside the illusion, but within it. Not after the illusion is destroyed, but as it is seen through. Not separate from you, but whispering through you. This real is not a thing — it is a knowing. It cannot be held, but it can be lived.

The eyes may never see it. But the soul remembers. And the heart recognizes its echo.

The Trinity of Soul, Self, and Creation

[see appendix A & B]

✦ Integrative Note:
The Trinity and the Five-Fold Human

The Trinity of **Soul, Self, and Creation** offers one way of seeing how reality itself moves—how essence flows into form and back again.

The **Five-Fold Human**—Body, Mind, Heart, Intuition, and Soul—offers another way of seeing how that movement lives *within us.*

Each framework is a lens. We use more than one not to complicate the path, but to study it from different angles. The trinity maps a *cosmic circuitry* of being; the five-fold map explores the *instrument* through which that circuitry is played.

✦ Book 1 Guiding Definitions

1. **The Soul — the Seed / Inner Spark**

    The soul is the quiet core of divinity within, the spark that remembers what is true even when the self forgets. Here in Book 1 we meet it as a seed beginning to stir beneath the soil of conditioning, sending the first rootlets of remembrance through the crust of habit and fear.

    (Simple view: the soul is the real "you," a seed of light starting to grow.)

2. **The Self — the Vehicle / Cocoon**
   The self is the composite of personality, identity, and ego shaped by family, culture, and circumstance.
   It is the vessel through which the soul experiences time. In early awakening we begin to notice that the self we thought was "me" is largely a reflection of the world's training—a protective cocoon waiting to open.
   (Simple view: the self is the spacesuit we've been wearing; awakening begins when we realize we are more than the suit.)

3. **Creation — the Total Field**
   Creation (***for this exploration***) is everything that is not the soul: the physical world, nature, society, relationships, and unseen forces that shape our experience. It is the living mirror in which the self learns and the soul recognizes itself.
   (Simple view: creation is the whole playground of life—everything around and within us that helps us wake up.)

Together they form the first circuit of becoming:
Soul initiates → Self translates → Creation resonates.

✦ Trinity Transitional Note

These three are not fixed categories but evolving ways of seeing. In our first glimpse of awakening, the self feels like a cocoon being reshaped, the soul like a seed awakening inside it, and creation (including world) like the vast classroom around us.

In Book Two: *The Self: A Soul Whisperer's Guide to Embodied Identity*, consciousness matures, **this same trinity reveals new dimensions**: the soul becomes a beam of living light, the self a prism through which that light refracts, and creation the luminous spectrum of expression that returns the song to its source.

If awakening reveals the illusion, then the path that follows is a sacred return — not to another doctrine or belief, but to what has always been quietly true. Once we see what is not real, the yearning begins for what is. We may not be able to name it, but we can feel it. It is not a thought. Not a role. Not a memory. It is something more ancient than all of that. A spark that has watched us dream, fall, rise, forget, and remember again. This is the soul.

The soul is not something to be gained or earned. It is not separate from us. It is who we are beneath all the layers we have mistaken for identity. And yet, paradoxically, it is also more than us — a fragment of the infinite, a unique tone in the great harmony of Source.

But the soul does not travel alone. It moves through a trinity — one that unites the eternal, the embodied, and the unfolding. This trinity is composed of soul, self, and creation.

> *"The freedom to be yourself is a gift only you can give yourself. But once you do, no one can take it away."* — Doe Zantamato

Together, they form the sacred circuitry through which truth comes into form.

To awaken is not simply to know the soul, but to allow the self to align with it and begin to express something true into the field of creation — not truth as an idea or ideal, but truth as being, as transmission, as conduit.

Authenticity, then, is not an act. It is not a curated version of ourselves. It is becoming transparent to the soul — of removing the blocks, the filters, the distortions that dim our inner light. It is allowing the self to become a vessel clear enough for the soul to shine through without resistance.

And when the soul's light radiates through the self and enters the world: Through word, thought, gesture, Love. It creates ripples of coherence in creation. Ripples that carry the unmistakable frequency, **Of something real.**

> You know it when you see it.
> You feel it in your bones.
> It doesn't need validation.
> It doesn't shout.
> It simply is.

> This is the divine circuitry of existence:
> Soul initiates.
> Self translates.
> Creation resonates.

And in that resonance, something sacred is remembered. Not taught, not learned — but recognized. Not imposed from above, but emerging from within.

To live from this trinity is to become a living transmission of truth. Not perfect. Not fixed. But real.

The Fivefold Map of Embodied Awakening

The Body: The Temple of Form
Archetypal Orientation

> *"The body is not a prison.*
> *It is the altar where the divine kneels to meet itself."*

The body is the sacred vessel of experience. It anchors the soul in space and time, gives us our senses, and carries the wisdom of every moment we've lived. More than flesh and bone, it is memory written in matter — bearing both the weight of old wounds and the keys to their release.

The body does not lie. While the mind may distort and the heart may withhold, the body speaks steadily in sensation, rhythm, contraction, and release. To honor the body is to welcome it not as obstacle, but as temple — the first altar on the path of awakening.

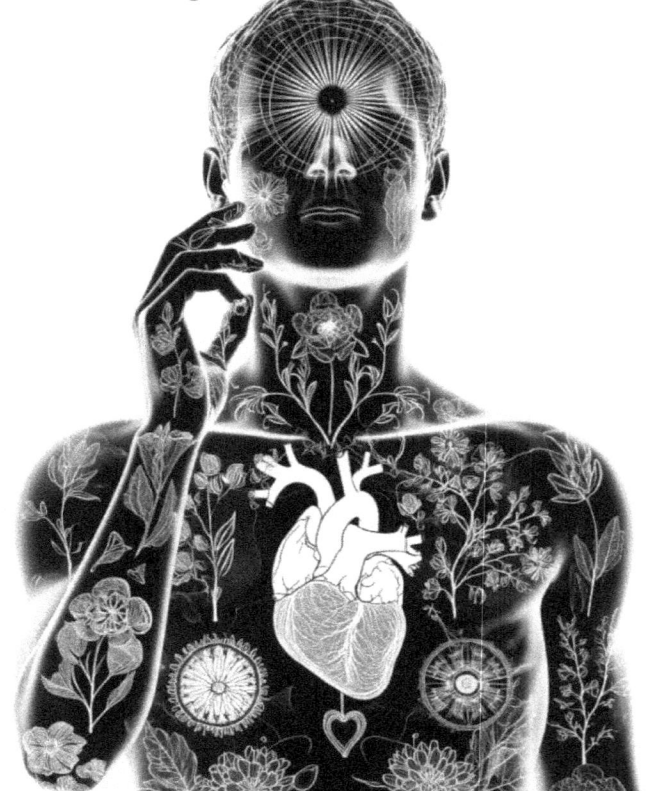

The Body's Map

- **Language**: sensation, posture, hunger, pleasure, pain, instinct
- **Gift**: embodied awareness, grounding, immediacy of being
- **Shadow**: numbness, disconnection, shame, addiction
- **Access Points**: breath, movement, stillness, embodied awareness
- **Awakening Pathways**: somatic intelligence, trauma release, practices of embodiment

Bringing the Body Online

To bring the body online is to come home to sensation — to feel again, without judgment. To welcome the tremble, the ache, the shiver, the fatigue, not as problems but as teachers. This is the beginning of reconciliation: to be in the body rather than at war with it.

Martial traditions remind us that the body is our first instructor. Through form, discipline, and flow, movement becomes prayer — precision and embodied presence fused. As in Aikido, we discover awakening not through resistance but through attunement.

In shamanic traditions, the body is called the drum of the spirit. Breath, heartbeat, and footsteps are sacred rhythms. To dance, to shake, to walk barefoot on the earth — these are not mere gestures, but ways of remembering wholeness.

The body is where awakening begins. It is the ground beneath us and the doorway through which every other dimension of awakening must pass.

The Mind: The Architect of Perception

"Thought creates the lens — but love opens the eyes."

The mind builds stories out of sensation and meaning out of memory. It imagines, compares, projects, and plans. It is the architect of perception — a tool that can design clarity or distortion. The mind is a powerful servant but a dangerous master. Left unchecked, it entangles us in inherited stories, looping thoughts, and compulsive judgments. But when awakened, it does not vanish — it becomes liberated from illusion.

The awakened mind does not
cling to certainty;
it learns to rest
in paradox.
It does not
force silence
but settles naturally
into clarity, like a lake
whose surface stills
to reflect what is.
Through the mind
we glimpse both
the limits of logic and
the doorways beyond it.

The Mind's Map

- **Language:** thought, belief, logic, expectation, projection
- **Gift:** discernment and vision
- **Shadow:** overthinking, distortion, attachment to story, control, spiritual bypass via intellect
- **Access Points:** inquiry, contemplation, spaciousness, paradox
- **Awakening Pathways:** examining conditioning and programming, questioning inherited stories, cultivating inner silence

Bringing the Mind Online

To bring the mind online is to question what we believe. To turn inward with courage and curiosity. To pull back the veil of inherited thought. To disentangle truth from programming.

The awakened mind is not loud — it is clear. It does not seek to conquer but to understand. In Buddhism, this is the beginning of right view: the recognition that thought is not reality itself. We do not trust every thought — we observe it. Through meditation, the mind is not silenced, but seen. Noise gives way to stillness; confusion to clarity.

In martial arts, the mind must be both alert and empty. The warrior knows: if the mind is crowded, the body hesitates. To be present is to be precise. This is *Mushin* — the no-mind state: calm, focused, fluid.

The mind, once a restless architect of illusions, becomes a clear mirror. Not a prison of thought, but a window for vision.

Heart: The Seat of Coherence

"Feeling is the soul's language before it finds words."

The heart is more than emotion — it is the center of compassion, courage, and coherence. It is the field where soul and self begin to align. The heart feels resonance before the mind can explain, and it responds with openness or contraction. In this way, the heart is both compass and bridge — measuring truth not in logic, but in the felt vibration of life itself.

To awaken through the heart is to allow grief, longing, and joy to become sacred expressions of the soul. The heart's vastness is not weakness but strength: its breaking is not an ending, but an opening. When the heart comes online, it restores the thread of connection between ourselves, others, and the greater whole.

The Heart's Map

- **Language:** feeling, resonance, longing, connection
- **Gift:** love and integration
- **Shadow:** guardedness, resentment, emotional overwhelm, repression, bypassing grief
- **Access Points:** gratitude, vulnerability, compassion, sacred honesty
- **Awakening Pathways:** emotional intelligence, heart coherence, energetic fields, soulful resonance

Bringing the Heart Online

To bring the heart online is to open to connection and truth. To feel what has been buried. To risk tenderness in a guarded world. To live in communion with life, with others, and with our own depth. The heart is not soft because it is weak — it is soft because it is vast. Its breaking is not the end — it is the beginning.

The Buddha taught compassion not as sentiment, but as liberation. Loving-kindness (*Metta*) dissolves the illusion of separation. To love, even when fear lingers, is the highest courage. The heart is not here to be protected, but to be expressed.

In shamanic tradition, the heart is the bridge between worlds. It carries the pulse of ancestors and the dreams of the unborn. It is the firekeeper of soul vision and human longing. The open heart is the medicine drum of the healer — beating with rhythm that restores coherence to all who listen.

The awakened heart is both anchor and horizon. It roots us in love while expanding us into the infinite.

Intuition: The Bridge Between Worlds

"Intuition is not a sixth sense — it is the first one we forgot."

Intuition is the whisper between dimensions — the subtle voice of knowing that bypasses the mind. It speaks through symbols, synchronicities, and quiet urgings. Intuition is not an extra sense tacked onto human experience; it is a primal current that once guided us before logic took the throne. When remembered, it becomes the compass that orients us toward alignment, weaving soul and self into a single thread of guidance.

The Intuition's Map

- **Language:** knowing, sensing, nudges, inner voices, symbols
- **Gift:** guidance and alignment
- **Shadow:** doubt, confusion, disconnection, reliance on external authority, fear of inner knowing
- **Access Points:** silence, receptivity, trust, inner listening
- **Awakening Pathways:** gut feelings, energetic truth, learning to listen without logic, cultivating intuitive trust

Bringing Intuition Online

To bring intuition online is to trust the unseen. To attune to whispers rather than shouts. To sense what is not spoken, yet deeply known. To move through life without always needing a map. Intuition is not a skill to develop but a reconnection to the thread of knowing that was never lost, only forgotten.

In Buddhist mysticism, insight (*prajna*) transcends logic. It is sudden, deep, and wordless — arriving in stillness, not strategy. Shamans walk between worlds with intuition as their compass. They read the wind, the fire, the flight of birds, knowing that the invisible is just as real as the seen. When the veil thins, intuition becomes vision.

In martial arts, intuition is reflex refined by embodied awareness. The master does not think — they sense. Movement arises from inner stillness, like a wave that knows when to strike and when to bow.

To live by intuition is to walk in rhythm with the unseen world, guided not by certainty but by trust.

Soul: The Eternal Spark

"The soul does not awaken to the world. It awakens from it."

The soul is the unchanging essence — a unique frequency of Source expressed through this human incarnation. It cannot be broken or diminished, only forgotten. The soul is not distant; it is simply quiet, waiting beneath our roles and reactions. To awaken is to remember the soul and allow it to live through the self — not as an abstract idea, but as the most intimate reality of who we are.

The soul is pure awareness: the eternal witness within, the one who holds memory across lifetimes, the keeper of sacred contracts and destiny threads. It arrives in moments of awe, stillness, and revelation — those times when we suddenly remember that life is not random, but radiant with meaning.

The Soul's Map

- **Language:** truth, calling, remembrance, purpose
- **Gift:** meaning and authenticity
- **Shadow:** forgetting, ego identification, amnesia, disconnection from purpose, existential despair
- **Access Points:** devotion, surrender, remembrance, stillness, sacred awareness
- **Awakening Pathways:** soul memory, sacred contracts, destiny, direct experiences of awe and stillness

Bringing the Soul Online

To bring the soul online is to embody divinity — not as a concept, but as an experience. The soul does not force its way forward; it waits patiently, like a quiet flame beneath the noise of personality. To bring it online is to let it lead — to let its grace move through flesh, thought, feeling, and will.

In shamanic healing, the soul is both essence and guide. When the soul is lost, illness follows. When the soul is returned, wholeness blooms. To embody soul is to walk with spirit in every step.

In Buddhism, the soul is glimpsed as the empty fullness of true nature. Beyond ego, beyond form, there is only *suchness*, pure being, undivided. Not separate, not personal, yet deeply intimate. To live from soul is to move as one with the whole.

In the martial way, the soul is not spoken but lived. It is the source behind the strike, the stillness behind the stance, the sacred essence that bows before and after every match — honoring the spirit in the other, and the greater field we both inhabit.

And as each aspect of the Fivefold awakens, they begin to converse. The mind no longer argues with the heart — it seeks its counsel. The body no longer numbs the soul — it expresses it. Intuition becomes a trusted guide, not a fleeting impulse. And the soul, no longer banished to the background, steps forward as conductor — orchestrating life not through force, but through resonance.

This is integration.
This is coherence.
This is the dance of the awakened.
This is the beginning of something real.

Bringing The Five Online

As each of the five awakens, something greater stirs within us. These aspects are not separate notes to be mastered in isolation — they are instruments tuning to one another, resonating into coherence.

The body offers its grounding, the mind its clarity, the heart its love, the intuition its guidance, and the soul its sacred essence, the eternal witness within. Together, they form a symphony of being.

Awakening does not end when one aspect comes alive. It deepens when they begin to move together — when sensation, thought, feeling, knowing, and presence align in rhythm. This is when life itself becomes prayer, not as ritual alone, but as the way we walk, breathe, and meet the world.

And so now ponder and turn to the question of alignment: What happens when all five sing as one?

Alignment — When All Bodies Sing

"When the body, mind, heart, intuition, and soul align we become a living prayer."

Awakening deepens not in isolation but in integration. Each aspect of the fivefold human carries its own intelligence, yet none are complete on their own. The body grounds us, the mind clarifies, the heart connects, the intuition guides, and the soul illuminates. But when they move together, something more is born — coherence.

Alignment is not perfection. It is rhythm. It is the ongoing practice of allowing these five voices to harmonize rather than compete. When they sing together, life itself becomes music — an embodied prayer, rising and falling with the breath of existence.

Alignment Map

- **Practices:** meditation, breath, ritual, silence, embodied awareness
- **Role of Rhythm:** balance, cycles, seasonal and lunar awareness, integration of rest and action
- **Embodied Expression:** living the awakened life in ordinary moments — how we walk, speak, love, and create
- **Shadow of Misalignment:** fragmentation, inner conflict, living in parts rather than whole

Bringing Alignment Online

To bring alignment online is to listen for the spaces between the notes. To notice when body, mind, heart, intuition, and soul are pulling in different directions — and to gently invite them back into dialogue. Alignment is less about control than about coherence; less about fixing than about attuning.

In contemplative practice, alignment is cultivated through rhythm — daily rituals of silence, prayer, or meditation that bring the inner world into order. In shamanic traditions, alignment is experienced in cycles — honoring the turning of seasons, the waxing and waning of the moon, the rhythm of earth itself. In martial arts, alignment is revealed in flow — the seamless coordination of stance, breath, and intention.

Alignment does not erase shadow, but integrates it. The guarded heart can soften into trust when the body feels safe. The restless mind can grow still when intuition leads. The weary soul can shine more fully when the heart and body carry its essence into form.

When all five bodies sing, we become more than ourselves. We become resonance. We become a living prayer — not in what we do alone, but in the way we are.

"Asato mā sad gamaya, tamaso mā jyotir gamaya, mṛtyor mā amṛtaṁ gamaya."
– Brihadaranyaka Upanishad 1.3.28

Lead me from the unreal to the Real,
Lead me from darkness to Light,
Lead me from death to Immortality.

Feeling, Emotion, and Inner Atmospheres

To awaken is to begin listening differently. And one of the most profound shifts in perception occurs when we learn to distinguish between emotion and feeling — two inner experiences often mistaken as one.

Emotion is like weather. It comes and goes, often without warning. It is reactive, tied to the stories we carry, the beliefs we hold, and the moments that catch us off guard. Emotions are the body's response to a triggered thought, a memory, or a stimulus from the outside world. They flare up like lightning storms — powerful, beautiful, and fleeting. In their shadow, they can overwhelm, distort, and pull us into loops of reactivity and confusion.

Feeling, however, is more like climate — the deeper atmospheric layer of our being. It does not spike in the same way, nor does it fade as quickly. Feelings are subtler, slower, more enduring. They emerge not from the mind's interpretations, but from the soul's quiet knowing. Feeling often arises in stillness, when the noise subsides and the deeper truth can surface without competition.

Emotions move through us, rising, cresting, and falling. Feelings move from us, they are expressions of our deeper being. Where emotion says, *"React now!"* driven by the urgency of pain, fear, or excitement, feeling says, *"Pause. Listen. Respond."* It asks for presence.

Emotion is often tangled with ego. It is the soundtrack of our conditioned perception, shaped by wounds and patterns we may not even be aware of. Feeling is aligned with essence. It is the resonance of the heart and soul, pointing us toward what's true even when the mind doesn't understand it.

"Emotion is the music of our current perception. Feeling is the melody of our becoming."

To navigate this distinction is to begin cultivating what we call inner atmosphere — the subtle energetic climate of the heart. This atmosphere is not fixed; it shifts with our healing, our choices, and our willingness to be present. A closed heart may storm with unprocessed emotions. An open heart begins to resonate with clarity, coherence, and compassion.

When our inner atmosphere clears, we become less reactive and more receptive. We stop being tossed by the winds of every passing thought or trigger. Instead, we begin to hear the whisper beneath the wind — the deeper guidance that comes not from fear, but from truth.

We begin to live not in reaction, but in resonance.

This is emotional maturity.
This is spiritual intelligence.
This is the subtle art of feeling our way home.

The Return to the Real

"Nothing real can be threatened. Nothing unreal exists.
Herein lies the peace of God."
— A Course in Miracles

What is *real?*

We often equate reality with what can be seen, touched, measured, or agreed upon — with what appears stable, provable, or repeatable. But awakening dismantles this assumption. It reveals that much of what we've called *real* has merely been *common*. Familiar. Rehearsed. Agreed upon by consensus but not necessarily born from truth.

Reality is not always what is most visible. Often, it is what remains when everything false falls away.

The journey of awakening is not just about seeing through illusion — it is about learning to trust what we find on the other side. And paradoxically, the *real* does not always come with the certainty we're used to. It does not shout. It does not insist. It does not carry the loud signatures of validation, social proof, or external achievement. Instead, the real arrives quietly — as a *resonance*, a recognition, a remembering.

"The real is not found in the concrete, but in the congruent — those moments when something within us and something beyond us suddenly agree."

Reality, in its most sacred sense, is not static. It is relational. It lives in the moments when our body, heart, mind, intuition, and soul come into *coherence* — when we are fully present, when our actions align with our inner truth, and when our essence is felt, not forced.

The real is not something we find *after* the illusion is destroyed. It is something we begin to *see through* the illusion. It is embedded in the ordinary — in a breath, a glance, a pause — when we are no longer pretending to be someone we're not.

Many spend lifetimes chasing what is *not real*: validation from systems that don't see their soul, love from people who don't recognize their essence, safety in roles that suffocate their truth. And even when they achieve these things, they are haunted by a quiet ache — the sense that something is missing, even in the midst of apparent success.

That ache is the soul's compass, nudging us back toward the real.

The *return to the real* is not a retreat from the world, but a deeper *participation* in it. It is the shedding of masks, not the abandonment of life. It is the reorientation of being — from outer display to inner truth.

To return to the real is to:

- **Honor the body.** Let it be your grounding place, the sacred instrument that anchors truth in form.
- **Witness the mind.** Not as enemy, but as translator. Not as master, but as companion.
- **Listen to heart.** Let it be the chamber of coherence, where decision and direction are felt before they are reasoned.
- **Trust intuition.** Let it be your compass when the map no longer makes sense.
- **Move from soul.** Not from habit or programming, but from the inner knowing that can't be explained — only honored.

This return is not a singular moment. It is a rhythm — a homecoming we revisit again and again, as layers of illusion fall and deeper truths emerge.

And this truth is not sterile or fixed. It is *alive*. It grows as we grow. It evolves as we evolve. It deepens as we deepen.

"Truth is not a possession but an inner knowing. It cannot be held, only lived."

To live from the real is not to be flawless. It is to be *faithful* to what is true — even when it's inconvenient, even when it costs us something, even when it asks us to surrender everything, we thought we were.

This is the sacred choreography of the awakened human. A life in motion, animated by something eternal.

Not perfect. Not performative. Not provable.
But unmistakably, undeniably true.
This… is something real.

*We stripped away illusion and glimpsed what remains
when all else falls—something real, something eternal.*

But to live from this truth is no small turning.

*The soul, once remembered, must now be embodied.
And this is where the path narrows.*

Because to carry the light… we must face the dark.

*As we continue, we now turn
toward the sacred descent—
where the soul is tempered,
and the self is undone.*

Chapter Four: The Dark Night of the Soul.

Chapter Four
The Dark Night of the Soul

"The dark night of the soul isn't just emotional, it's cognitive dissonance at the deepest level. It's when your mind can no longer explain your reality, your beliefs no longer fit your experience, and your identity begins to crack under the weight of truth. It's not madness— it's metamorphosis."

The Dark Night as the Realization of Disconnection

*The true darkness is not the absence of light—
but the sudden awareness that you have been walking in shadow for longer than you dared admit.*

*It is not simply the grief of God's silence— it is the breaking recognition that **you stopped listening** long ago.*

It is not just a season of sorrow— it is a sacred reckoning, a collapse of the illusion that you were ever truly awake while you went through the motions of meaning.

*The Dark Night does not always arrive as suffering— it often comes as **a mirror**. Not one that reflects who you are, but one that reveals **how far you've wandered** from who you were created to be.*

*And in that reflection, you do not see punishment. You see **a lifeline**.*

Because it is in the seeing, in the sudden, searing awareness of your disconnection— that the path Home begins.

Not because God returns, but because you finally noticed you had turned your face away.

"In the dark night of the soul, bright flows the river of God."
— St. John of the Cross

There comes a moment on the path of awakening when the lights go out—not in the world, but within. The familiar glow of clarity fades. Meaning unravels. Once-anchored truths loosen their grip. The voice of the Divine, so once near and luminous, now becomes still, distant, or even silent.

It doesn't come in thunder or flame. It comes quietly, like a tide slipping out to sea, leaving you standing alone on the shore of your inner life.

The soul begins to stir—not in ecstasy, but in exile. Not in certainty, but in surrender. And the self—the fragile identity assembled from culture, conditioning, memory, and survival—no longer fits the shape of your becoming.

What you called "you" begins to tremble. Not because something has gone wrong, but because something deeper is waking up.

The self is not who you are. It is the vehicle—a collection of roles, masks, stories, and strategies—built to navigate a programmed world.

But there is something ancient within you that cannot be programmed. Something eternal that cannot be conditioned. Something holy that cannot be improved —only revealed.

And when the soul, long hidden in the backseat, prepares to take the wheel, the vehicle of the self begins to break down. Not as punishment, but as sacred necessity.

The ego cannot guide where the soul intends to go.
The mask cannot breathe in the air of truth.

Like the caterpillar dissolving in the chrysalis,
everything that once defined you begins to melt.
Not into nothing, but into essence.

The soul is not created through this process—it is unveiled.
The self dissolves, the way a shell must crack for the seed to sprout.

This is the dark night.

It is not a detour.
It is not a mistake.
It is not regression,
punishment,
or failure.

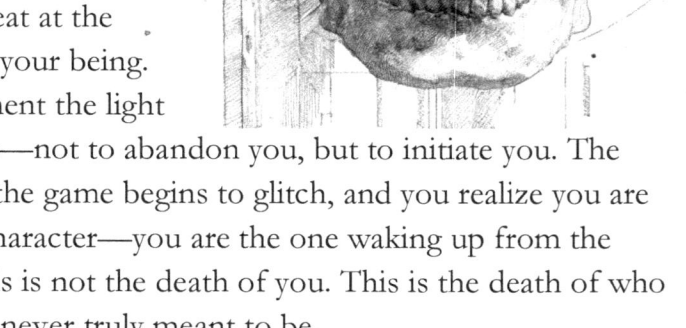

It is the moment
the soul reclaims its
rightful seat at the
center of your being.
The moment the light
goes dark—not to abandon you, but to initiate you. The moment the game begins to glitch, and you realize you are not the character—you are the one waking up from the story. This is not the death of you. This is the death of who you were never truly meant to be.

And what is coming…is real.

The Collapse of False Identity

"My barn having burned down, I can now see the moon."
— Mizuta Masahide

Awakening does not begin with clarity.
It begins with collapse.

Not a collapse of the world around you,
but of the world within you—
the one built from stories, expectations, and roles
you didn't even know you were performing.

The identity you've worn—stitched together from praise
and pain, forged in the fires of survival, polished by
appearances, validated by applause—
begins to lose its shape.

You feel it at first as discomfort.
The tightness of a mask you can no longer keep on.
The awkwardness of a role that once fit like skin, now
sliding off like armor you forgot how to carry.

The personality, the ego, the curated self-image—
these were not false in their intent,
but they are not true in their essence.

They were vehicles—built to drive through the world of
appearance. Constructs. Costumes. Interfaces. Crafted to
survive, to belong, to succeed.
Necessary once… but not eternal.

And now, the soul within you—long quiet, long waiting—is
beginning to rise.

And so, the scaffolding begins to fall.
The mirrors you once used to see yourself crack under the pressure of becoming.
The accolades that once made you feel whole now ring hollow. The relationships built on projection tremble with the weight of truth.

This is not failure. It is sacred disassembly.

This is the falling away of what was never truly you.

The false self doesn't die in fire—it dissolves in honesty. This is not the end of you, but the beginning of the you who never had to perform to be loved.

What collapses is not your worth.
It is the illusion that your worth had to be earned.

This is the beginning of the great remembering—
that you are not the self you built… You are the soul that has been housed within it all along.

And that soul, now awakening, does not seek improvement. It seeks expression. It seeks truth.

The Absence of Light as Grace

*"Darkness is not the absence of light —
it is the womb of it."* — JaiViibes

One of the most disorienting initiations in the dark night is the loss of divine familiarity.

The signs stop showing up.
The synchronicities dry out.
The guidance that once arrived in whispers or dreams…
disappears.
The inner voice that once stirred like wind through the soul falls silent.
The warmth of connection becomes a memory.

It can feel like exile. It can feel like God has gone.

But what if this absence is not abandonment,
but refinement?

What if the silence is not punishment,
but preparation?

What if the very absence you fear
is the container being carved for a deeper arrival?

Grace sometimes wears the mask of distance
because proximity would still be clung to like proof.

The soul is being asked to walk not by confirmation,
but by communion.

The light withdraws, not to torment you,
but to initiate you into a love that does not depend on sensation.

> *"When it is dark enough, you can see the stars."*
> *— Martin Luther King Jr.*

This is when your spiritual senses, once led by sweetness,
are stripped of their sugar…
so you may taste the bitter root of truth.

This is not the withdrawal of the Divine—
it is the drawing inward of the soul.

The hiddenness of God is the deepening of devotion.

The fire is no longer outside you.
It is being moved within.

To remain in this stillness— to pray when no one seems to listen, to trust when all signs are gone, to love when you feel nothing— is the essence of holy maturity.

This is love without bargain.
This is faith without spectacle.
This is devotion that needs no reward.

This is where soul replaces self at the altar.

This is where you stop reaching for proof and become the being you once sought.

Spiritual Despair as Sacred Ground

"The soul would have no rainbow if the eyes had no tears."— Native American Proverb

It may look like depression. It may feel like numbness, meaninglessness, or exhaustion that words cannot reach.

But what if this isn't a breakdown, but a breaking open?

What if the void you're staring into
is not an end,
but a womb?

This is not the death of the soul.
This is the place where the soul begins to germinate.

Despair is not failure.
It is the ache of the self being peeled away.
It is the slow disintegration of everything you built to protect the soul from fully being seen.

You are not unraveling because something has gone wrong.
You are unraveling because the truth is emerging—
and it no longer fits inside the shell of who you used to be.

This is the deep tilling of the inner ground.
This is the inner winter that prepares for a spring not yet imagined.

All that is false, conditioned, secondhand, inherited…
is being loosened from your roots.

And the pain you feel—
that quiet ache behind your eyes,
that restless emptiness in your chest—
is not proof of spiritual death.

It is the pressure of becoming.

The seed does not break because it fails.
It breaks because it is ready.
Ready to become something it has never been before.

The collapse of meaning is not your enemy.
It is the clearing of space for authentic meaning to emerge—
not borrowed, not taught, not inherited—
but revealed through your own becoming.

This is not a mistake.
This is metamorphosis.

This is the sacred darkness where the miracle begins.
The place where surrender is the only prayer left,
and still, something stirs in the soil.

You are not falling apart.
You are falling through—
into the unseen hands that are catching you from within.

Detachment as Initiation

> *"Anything you cannot relinquish when it has outlived its usefulness possesses you."*— Peace Pilgrim

People fade. Passions fizzle. The things that once lit you up now flicker, dim, and go out. The pleasures that used to bring you joy turn to dust on the tongue. The dreams you once chased with urgency now feel weightless—like echoes from a life you no longer live.

This is detachment—but not the cold withdrawal of abandonment.

This is initiation.

The soul is beginning to take the wheel, and everything tethered to the old identity—the conditioned self, the survival persona, the programmed path—begins to loosen and fall away.

You are not losing your life.
You are shedding the self that clung to it.

The roles you once played.
The desires that once defined you.
The opinions that shaped your choices.
The relationships built on show or projection…

They are not being stolen. They are being released—
because they no longer align with the soul that is awakening through you.

You may feel unmoored, drifting, untethered. And yes, it can feel like death.

But death is only frightening to what refuses to transform.

The truth is: you are being refined. You are being pared down to essence. And what remains… is what has always been real.

Only the soul is meant to stay.

What is false cannot follow.
What is real cannot be lost.

This is not the soul abandoning the self.
This is the soul no longer allowing itself to be buried beneath it.

The Ego's Surrender

"Surrender is not giving up something you don't want. It's letting go of something you've been holding onto that no longer works."
— Guy Finley

The ego does not surrender easily. It was built to survive, to solve, to strive. And so, it does what it knows best:

It fights the silence.
It negotiates with the dark.
It tries to spiritualize the suffering, make it meaningful, make it useful.

It scrambles for a lesson.
It reaches for a ritual.
It clings to a map.

It tries to fix what was never broken— only stripped of illusion.

It tries to produce progress from a process meant only for protection.

But the soul cannot be managed. It cannot be manipulated, optimized, or rushed.

And so, eventually, the strategies fail.

The affirmations lose their spark.
The journal pages fall blank.
The rituals feel empty.
The stories of who you were and where you're going no longer hold weight.

And in this sacred exhaustion, something ancient and holy begins to happen. The self finally stops trying to save itself. Not because it gave up, but because it finally gave in.

This is not failure.
This is liberation.
This is not the end of you.
This is the end of the you that had to hold it all together.

The ego does not dissolve in one great ceremony. It dissolves in slow, quiet moments of emptiness that reveal their grace only in hindsight. This is the moment the self finally steps aside — not in shame, but in reverence.

Not because it was wrong, but because it was never meant to lead. And into that quiet space, the soul steps forward. Not as a conqueror, but as eternal awareness.
A remembering.
A homecoming.

The Self Realigns as the Soul Emerges

"You will be lost and unlost over and over again. Relax, love. You were meant to be this glorious, Epic, Story."
— Nayyirah Waheed

Once the self has been humbled by silence,
softened by surrender,
and emptied of the need to lead—
the soul begins to rise.

Not in a blaze of glory,
but in a quiet return to the center.

The compass of your being begins to shift.
It no longer points toward performance, validation, or survival.
It now turns inward—toward presence, authenticity, and alignment.

This is the beginning of the New Self.

Not a shinier version of the old self.
Not a spiritually decorated ego wearing robes of righteousness.
But a soul-embodied expression—
a self-made spacious and sincere, moved not by fear or approval,
but by truth and love.

The old self does not disappear.
It is reoriented.

It becomes a servant rather than a master. An instrument rather than an identity.

The personality, the body, the mind, the voice— they don't dissolve…they realign.

The self becomes the vehicle. The soul becomes the driver. You do not become less human. You become more whole. More grounded. More alive. You stop asking, "Who am I supposed to be?" and begin to ask, "What wants to move through me?"

The mind yields to knowing beyond thought. The heart opens not from need, but from overflow. And life becomes a conversation between form and formlessness, between the visible self and the invisible soul that breathes it into being.

This is not becoming someone new. This is becoming who you always were—beneath the story, beneath the scaffolding, beneath the striving.

You are not being erased. You are being rewritten from the inside out.

And what emerges is not a self that seeks to prove its worth— but a self that lives as the expression of what is already whole.

Unknowing as Transformation

"The dark night is God's way of letting you walk into yourself." — Thomas Moore

The mind reaches for certainty. It searches for clarity like a torch in the night, trying to make sense of what cannot be contained in thought.

It wants a map. A plan. A promise that all of this ache will lead somewhere familiar.

But awakening does not bring certainty. It brings mystery. Everything you thought you knew begins to dissolve— not in rebellion, but in reverence.

What once seemed obvious now feels foreign. What once gave you confidence now crumbles in your hands. Even your beliefs about God, truth, identity, and purpose are placed on the sacred altar of unknowing.

The mind—once the loudest voice—grows quiet, because it no longer holds the answers.

The map disappears. The compass spins. And you are left in a vast, holy unknowing.

This is not the mind's failure.
This is the soul's invitation.

The soul does not teach through concepts.
It teaches through patient witnessing.

It speaks in stillness, in intuition, in deep resonances that require no explanation.

The paradox of transformation is this: you do not become something new. You become something eternal.

Something untouched by language.
Something unreachable by thought.
Something that has always been here,
beneath the veil of what you thought you knew.

This is not forgetting.
This is unlearning—a sacred shedding of illusion.

And to the mind, this can feel like death. But to the soul, this is homecoming.

To release the need to know
is to open the door to wisdom.

To stop grasping for understanding
is to be touched by truth.

You are not lost.
You are becoming spacious enough
to hold the Infinite.

Feeling Forsaken: The Christ Parallel

"When you feel forsaken, it is not because God has left—but because your soul is passing through the veil that separates belief from being."
— Thomas Merton (inspired phrasing, though not a direct quote)

There may come a moment so silent, so hollow, so stripped of all comfort and connection, that you feel utterly forsaken. Not metaphorically. Not theologically. But viscerally—like the ground beneath your soul has vanished and even God has turned away.

Even Christ, in his final hour, hanging between heaven and earth, cried out with a voice broken by pain and abandonment:

This is the soul's cry through the broken self. The self that has been emptied of identity, stripped of control, and rendered defenseless in the face of mystery.

It is the sound of a soul that has walked through every door and found no answers. It is the prayer that comes not from belief, but from being undone.

But what if this forsakenness is not the end? What if it is the final veil before union?

The silence you feel is not the absence of God— it is the collapse of the self's ability to perceive God.

The proximity of the Divine becomes unbearable to the old self, so it interprets nearness as absence. It confuses the intimacy of connection with the pain of invisibility.

But beneath the silence, beneath the ache, beneath the unbearable stillness…

The soul is almost home.

The Divine is not far away.
The Divine is within breath, closer than thought, pressing into you so intimately that the old self cannot find its edges anymore.

This is the surrender of separation. The end of needing to feel the Light in order to know you are held by it.

The veil is thinning. The ego is unraveling. And what feels like abandonment is, in truth, the moment before you remember:
You were never alone.

The Alchemy of Suffering

"Although the world is full of suffering, it is also full of the overcoming of it."— Helen Keller

Suffering does not strip the soul. It reveals it. Not by erasing what is false, but by burning it away.

Every wound becomes a portal.
Every heartbreak, an opening.
Every tear that falls without answer becomes a silent baptism—an initiation into a deeper truth that can only be known through the language of pain.

The old self does not survive the fire,
but something eternal does.

Suffering is not a failure in your spiritual journey. It is the forge in which the soul is tempered, refined, and made radiant.

The pain you feel is not a punishment— it is the pressure of transformation. It is life insisting that something old must end so something real can begin.

This is where the armor cracks.
This is where the acting ends.
This is where the soul, long buried beneath layers of striving, finally begins to shine through.

The story you once told yourself collapses, and in its place, something unspeakable is born.

Pain becomes prayer.
Loss becomes longing.
Longing becomes love—
not a love that clings,
but a love that knows.

A love that doesn't need to possess,
but simply radiates.

This is sacred alchemy.

This is soul fire.

The kind of fire that doesn't destroy what is essential,
but purifies it.

You are not being broken.
You are being broken open.

And what spills out is not weakness—
but light.

From Darkness to Devotion

"True devotion begins when the soul continues to love even in the absence of light."— Sister Vandana Mataji

Devotion is not born in ecstasy.
It is born in emptiness.

Not in the spiritual high, but in the hollow ache where all light seems to have gone out. It is forged not in the joy of receiving, but in the choice to remain faithful when there is nothing left to receive.

This is the place beyond miracles. Beyond answers. Beyond the signs and wonders you once clung to.

When there is no voice from heaven,
no divine glow, no synchronicity to reassure you…
and still— you stay.

Still, you love.
Still, you trust.
Still, you walk.

This is where real
devotion begins.
It is not a feeling.
It is a vow.

A soul-deep promise to remain true to the truth,
even when truth hides its face.

To say yes to the path
even when
the path is made
of fog and silence.

To keep the altar lit
when the flame has vanished.

This is not spiritual discipline.
This is sacred intimacy.

This is the soul choosing to love
God not for what is felt, but for what is
unseen, unspoken, unshakable.

This is the turning point. The moment
where the soul, once buried deep within
the architecture of the self, begins to
emerge. Not as an idea, but as the driver
of your life. The self steps back. The soul
steps forward.

And what moves through you now is not
effort, but essence. Not striving, but surrender.

Devotion is the choice to stay.
Even when you can't see.
Even when you can't hear.
Even when every part of you aches to turn back.

To stay is to become the light you once sought.

And that…
is holy.

The Threshold of Integration

"I am not what happened to me, I am what I choose to become."
— Carl Gustav Jung

The dark night is not an end.
It is an initiation.

It is not the closing of a chapter.
It is the doorway between worlds.
A sacred passage between who you were,
and who you are now ready to become.

You do not emerge with the same name.
You do not return to the same story.

You emerge carrying the same light—
but now, it is revealed.
Now, it leads.
Now, it lives through you.

What was shattered did not break you.
It made space for something sacred.
A connection. A purity. A knowing too deep for words.

The self—the performer, the protector, the architect of personality—
is no longer in charge.

It has not been erased.
It has been realigned.

It has become the servant of the soul.

And this is the real miracle.
Not that you made it through,
but that you've been reborn in truth.

You did not just survive the fire—
you let it remake you.

You did not just endure the emptiness—
you let it teach you how to be filled from within.

Now you walk forward,
not as the old self improved,
but as the soul embodied.

You carry the wisdom of the night within your chest.
You speak not from theory,
but from the ground of your own transformation.

You are not just healed.
You are hallowed.

The ache has become your compass.
The silence has become your song.
The darkness has become the cradle of your becoming.

You have crossed the threshold.
You are not who you were.

And now—
everything real begins.

We have walked through the night with no stars.
We have cried out to the silence,
touched the bottom of the unknowing,
and discovered that even in forsakenness,
we are never truly alone.

The dark night did not destroy us.
It dissolved us.
It unmade the self
so the soul could rise.

Now, from this stripped and sacred ground,
we begin again—not as the one who seeks,
but as the one who sees.

As we continue,
we turn now toward a deeper
exploration of awakening—
not as a concept, but as a living reality
unfolding from within.

Chapter Five: A Deeper Exploration of Awakening.

Awakening
Part 2

Chapter Five
Deeper Exploration of Awakening

"Planted within the soil of your heart, love and peace is what makes the growing start. Sunshine and water... and someday you'll know."
— I Am a Seed, JaiViibes

Introduction

Awakening is often spoken of as an inner journey — a path inward to the truth that was always there. And this is true. But it is also, simultaneously, a great *unfolding*.

Like a seed nestled in the darkness beneath the soil, something within us begins to stir. But it does not stir alone. The warmth of the sun, the nourishment of rain, the breath of air — these outer forces interact with the hidden potential inside. It is not the seed alone that causes growth, nor the sun alone that brings life. It is their sacred *meeting* — the outer activating the inner, the inner reaching for the outer.

So, it is with the soul.

Awakening is both *inward activation* and *outward emergence*. A spiraling journey that goes in both directions — one that draws us deep into the chambers of the self, and one that draws the self out into the world, transformed.

This is not a linear process. Nor is it fully known. The conditions that support awakening — stillness, feeling, suffering, love, loss, devotion — are often visible. But the inner unfolding, the moment when the shell of self begins to crack, the divine timing of soul emergence — that remains mysterious. Sacred. God-given.

And yet, in this chapter, we try to illuminate what we can. To name the contours of our becoming. To give language to what is often felt but not spoken. To create a map — not to contain the mystery, but to walk alongside it.

We begin with the recognition that the human being is not one thing, but many. That we awaken not through mind alone, but through *layers of being* — the body, the mind, the heart, the intuition, and the soul. Each one its own seed. Each one capable of breaking open. Each one waiting for the right conditions to bloom.

In the pages that follow, we honor both what we can name and what we cannot. We explore the anatomy of awakening not to dissect it, but to more fully *participate in its unfolding*.

This is the deeper awakening — the one that doesn't just reveal what is inside, but invites it to *become*.

Physical Awakening
Body - Nervous System - Survival Awareness

Part One reveals the body as temple and teacher, the altar where spirit takes form. Part Two turns to the lived body of nerves, fascia, and breath — where survival imprints and somatic memory become the first thresholds of awakening.

The Body: Portal of Awakening

Practical and Psychological Depth

"The body remembers what the story forgets."

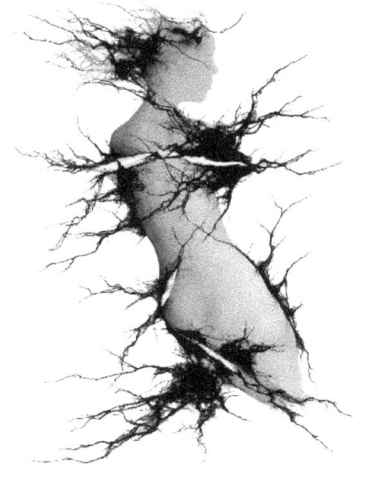

Before the mind spins its narratives or the soul whispers its symbols, the body is already listening.
It is the first to hold.
The first to brace.
The first to tremble beneath the weight of experience.
A shallow breath.
A clenched jaw.
A racing heart in stillness.
These are not failures — they are signals.
The body speaks in fascia, muscle, gut, and nerve, offering us the first doorway into awakening.

The Body as Portal

To awaken physically is to recognize that the body is not a barrier to the spiritual path — it *is* the path. We were never meant to transcend the body, but to inhabit it fully. Not by escaping sensation, but by breathing into it. Not by rejecting flesh, but by revering it as a vessel of spirit.

Awakening begins below:

- in the jaw that tenses,
- in the shoulders that collapse,
- in the belly that knots,
- in the pelvic floor that braces.

These are not random discomforts; they are the archives of what we were never taught to feel. To awaken through the body is to allow what has been held in silence to unfold.

The Nervous System: Keeper of Memory

The nervous system is the bridge between survival and spirit. Fight, flight, freeze, fawn — these are not only psychological patterns, but physiological imprints etched into our cells.

- When we were unsafe, the body adjusted.
- When we were unseen, the body hid.
- When we were silenced, the body stored it away.

Awakening here requires listening, not overriding. Regulation is not weakness — it is resurrection. The same systems that absorbed trauma also carry the capacity for healing.

As Bessel van der Kolk observes:
"Trauma is not just an event that took place sometime in the past; it is also the imprint left by that experience on mind, brain, and body."

This imprint often becomes the first threshold of awakening: a disruption that pushes us back toward embodiment.

Signals of Physical Awakening

Awakening in the body often begins as disturbance before it reveals itself as renewal. Signals may include:

- Sudden awareness of posture, tension, or breath.
- A pull toward stillness, grounding, or deep rest.
- Old injuries resurfacing somatically.
- Heightened sensitivity to food, sound, light, or touch.
- Growing discomfort with overstimulation or disembodied living.

These are not regressions — they are recalibrations. The body reorganizing itself toward wholeness.

The Shadow of Disembodiment

Disembodiment is more than personal neglect; it is a cultural condition. We are taught to push through, to numb pain, to prioritize achievement over being in the now. Mantras like *"tough it out"* or *"mind over matter"* erode our capacity to listen to the body's wisdom.

Over time, this disconnection creates a split: we live in our heads, dissociated from the ground of our being. The cost is anxiety, burnout, and estrangement from the present moment. To return to the body is to return to the now. And when we are in the now, the soul can finally speak clearly through us.

Dimensions of Awakening:
BODY - The Gate of Sensation and Survival

"The body tells the truth before the story does."

The body is the drumbeat of awakening — the first to feel, the last to lie. It reacts before the mind can explain, and remembers what the story forgets.

- **Shock**
  When everything familiar crumbles — accidents, trauma, betrayal — the body absorbs what the psyche cannot. This is not yet clarity, but disruption; not truth, but the breaking of illusion's container.
- **Flow State**
  The moment the dancer becomes the dance. Time dissolves. There is no "you" doing, only doing. Grace moving through flesh, a glimpse of embodiment.
- **Altered State (Somatic)**
  Fasting, breathwork, ecstatic movement — when the body is pushed beyond its habitual rhythm, doorways open. The ego loosens, the veil thins. Not every altered state is awakening, but many clear a path toward it.
- **Near-Death Experience**
  The body meets its edge; the curtain lifts. Many return with stories of light, peace, and life-review. Death becomes a reluctant usher, sometimes even a teacher.

- **Sacred Silence (Bodily Stillness)**
  Stillness not as absence but as presence. The body quiets, yet within the quiet there is a holy pulse. This is not numbness — it is the peace that passes understanding.

Somatic Practices for Awakening

Awakening through the physical body is not about fixing but befriending. These practices are invitations to relationship:

- **Breathwork:** Meeting life at its threshold.
- **Somatic experiencing:** Following sensation with compassion, allowing stuck energy to move.
- **Grounding rituals:** Walking barefoot, touching earth, anchoring into the present.
- **Yoga and sacred movement:** Not just going thru the motions, but for deep connected awareness.
- **Body scanning and conscious rest:** Learning the contours of our own vessel.

Each of these is a prayer in motion — a way of reclaiming safety and intimacy with the body.

Body's Invitation:
Feel what's true—before you try to name it.

Reflection

The body is the first altar.
When we learn to bow there
to listen to the signals,

to soften into sensation,
to trust the breath
we begin to return.
Not upward.
Not outward.
But inward and downward
into the root.

From there, the rest can rise.

Mental Awakening
Mind - Belief Systems - Thought Awareness

"You must first understand your conditioning to be free of it." — J. Krishnamurti

Part One shows the mind as architect of perception, capable of vision or illusion. Part Two brings us into the terrain of thought patterns, conditioning, and belief systems — where discernment arises by loosening the grip of the inner narrator.

The mind is a brilliant architect — able to build worlds from memory, imagination, logic, and belief. It is also the greatest illusionist. It can convince us that we are separate. It can reinforce false identities. It can cloak pain in thought loops so thick, we forget to feel.

To awaken mentally is to begin noticing the walls — and realizing they were painted by the hand of our own thinking.

This is the moment we look inward and begin to ask,
Whose voice is this?
Whose story am I living?"
It is the beginning of disentangling truth from programming. The birth of discernment.

The Thought Matrix

Most people do not think — they repeat.
The mind, left unchecked, recycles yesterday's fears, ancestral imprints, and inherited scripts from culture, religion, education, and family.

To awaken mentally is to begin to observe thought without becoming it.
To witness the stream without being swept away by the current.
To realize that **belief is not the same as truth**.

This awakening is often catalyzed by crisis or contradiction.
A moment when the story we've clung to no longer holds.
When what we thought was certain begins to crumble.

This is not a loss — it is a liberation.

> *"The mind is a wonderful servant, but a terrible master."*
> *— Old Proverb*

The Inner Narrator: Deconstructing the Voice

There is a voice inside, constantly narrating — interpreting, judging, analyzing.
It is not always kind. It is not always true.

But we mistake it for ourselves.

Mental awakening asks us to become *curious* about this voice.

- Is it my mother's worry?
- My father's shame?
- A religion's rulebook?
- A society's lie?

What we discover is that **the voice is many voices**, layered through time.

Awakening doesn't require we destroy the mind. It asks that we **take the microphone back**.

To shift from autopilot to awareness.

To turn monologue into dialogue.

To learn to think *with* the soul, not in place of it.

Signs of Mental Awakening

- Sudden clarity or insight after long confusion
- Questioning deeply held beliefs or identities
- Realization of thought patterns and unconscious assumptions

- Breakdowns in certainty, often followed by awe or humility
- A hunger for truth, philosophy, wisdom, and paradox

These are not signs of madness. They are signs of mental rebirth.

The Shadow of Mental Awakening

When awakening first fractures our mental constructs, it feels as though we've glimpsed behind reality's curtain. Ideas and beliefs once solid now appear as ephemeral shapes. This realization, both exhilarating and destabilizing, ignites a hunger for understanding.

Yet herein lies a subtle danger—the shadow of mental awakening. The mind, liberated from old dogmas, swiftly erects new intellectual fortresses, substituting old beliefs with refined, yet equally limiting frameworks. This trap of intellectual bypassing mistakes insight for embodiment, replacing lived truth with abstract concepts.

We navigate endless corridors of thought, entranced by abstraction, risking detachment from the body's immediacy, the heart's intuitive wisdom, and simple presence.

True awakening lies not in accumulating insights but in shedding illusions, not in intellectual conquest but quiet humility. Wisdom emerges from balancing knowing with not-knowing, holding paradox gently. The awakened mind must stay tethered to humility, heart, and body, or it risks becoming sterile.

Dimensions of Awakening:
MIND - The Architect of Meaning and Belief

*"When the mind finally bows,
it becomes a doorway instead of a wall."*

The mind seeks order. It searches for patterns, answers, frameworks. But in moments of awakening, the mind does more than analyze—it collapses, reforms, and sees anew.

- **Realization**
  The lightbulb moment. When a new truth reshapes a long-held pattern. It may be intellectual, but it rattles the whole scaffolding. It's not always awakening—but it clears the fog.
- **Epiphany**
  When logic and meaning collide in a burst of insight. The puzzle of life suddenly rearranges itself—and for a moment, you understand. Your mind is not just thinking—it's seeing.
- **Cognitive Dissonance**
  The friction between belief and reality. You feel it like a knot in your gut: *This isn't right. This doesn't fit anymore.* This ache is sacred. It signals readiness for evolution.
- **Revelation (Conceptual)**
  An idea so vast it arrives as a download. You didn't arrive at it—it arrived at you. It may be divine, it may be emergent—but it expands the map.
- **Witnessing (Mental Detachment)**
  When the mind steps back from itself. Thoughts arise, but they no longer define. You become the sky behind the storm.

Practices of Mental illumination

- **Mindfulness meditation**: Observing thoughts without attachment
- **Inquiry**: Asking, "Is this true? Who would I be without this thought?"
- **Journaling**: Externalizing the mind to better see its structure
- **Reading sacred or philosophical texts**: Introducing higher thought forms
- **Silence**: Creating space for original insight to emerge

"Do not believe in anything simply because you have heard it. Believe nothing unless it agrees with your own reason and your own common sense." — The Buddha

Mental awakening is not about emptying the mind
It's about reclaiming it.
It is about teaching the mind to serve the soul.
To think in alignment with the heart.
To imagine in harmony with the body.
To quiet itself so intuition can speak.

Mind's Invitation:
Look again—there is more to see.

Reflection

*The mind is not the enemy.
It is a garden. And like any garden, it must be tended.
Thoughts that no longer serve must be gently pruned.
New seeds — of wonder, spaciousness, and higher
vision — must be planted.*

*To awaken mentally is to reclaim authorship
of our inner narrative.
It is to realize: I am not the thought.
I am the awareness of thought.
And from that place, we begin
to write a new story*

— not from fear, but from soul.

Emotional Awakening
Heart - Feeling - Emotional Literacy

"The walls built to protect yourself became the same walls that kept you from love." — Mark Groves

If Part One reveals the archetypal role of the heart as bridge and healer, Part Two brings us into the lived experience of feeling — where love, grief, and vulnerability become doorways of psychological and somatic awakening.

The heart is not just a symbol.
It is a portal.
It is where the soul touches the world and feels it all.
Where sorrow becomes sacred.
Where joy breaks us open.
Where the language of awakening is not spoken, but felt.

To awaken emotionally is not to learn how to feel — it is to *remember that you were never meant to forget.*

It is to allow the tidal currents of grief, longing, love, and tenderness to rise — not as problems to fix, but as signals of aliveness.

The Intelligence of Feeling

Emotions are not intrusions. They are invitations. They arise not to derail our path but to illuminate it. Each feeling is a compass. Anger: a call to boundary. Grief: a signal of loss and love. Joy: alignment. Fear: a protector seeking safety. Shame: an echo of past wounds needing compassion.

"Feeling is the soul's first language — it speaks before thought, before words, before story."— JaiViibes

To truly awaken emotionally, we must meet each feeling without judgment, learning to decode their messages with care and curiosity. Feelings, when listened to deeply, reveal hidden truths about our inner landscape, guiding us toward healing, authenticity, and wholeness. Emotional wisdom comes from embracing vulnerability, allowing our hearts to break open, not apart. When we welcome all feelings as teachers rather than obstacles, they become gateways to deeper self-awareness and profound inner transformation.

Emotional awakening is not about constant happiness. It is about honesty. Emotional honesty. Heart integrity.

The Breaking Open

There is always a moment when the heart cracks. Sometimes softly. Sometimes violently. A betrayal. A death. A goodbye. A sudden wave of beauty. The ego cannot prepare for it. The mind cannot protect from it. It comes as if from nowhere — and suddenly, we are *feeling everything*.

This is the soul's entry point. Where we stop performing emotion and start *being moved*.

We cry without knowing why.
We love without needing a reason.
We grieve what was never ours, and somehow it frees us.

This is not weakness. This is what it means to be truly *human*.

"Out of suffering have emerged the strongest souls."
— Kahlil Gibran

Signs of Emotional Awakening

- Increased sensitivity or vulnerability
- Sudden weeping or laughter without explanation
- Emotional flashbacks or layered grief rising from the past
- A feeling of the heart "opening" or becoming more permeable
- The desire to express love, truth, and care more freely

These are the soul's fingerprints on the heart.

The Shadow of Emotional Awakening

Emotion can feel overwhelming. Like a storm with no edge. For those who have been taught to numb, to perform, or to hide — the floodgates opening can feel like drowning.

But every emotion, fully felt, has an edge. A rhythm. A wave. We are not meant to control emotion, nor to be consumed by it — but to **dance with it**. To let it speak, without letting it steer.

There is also the shadow of emotional over-identification — becoming the emotion, rather than witnessing it as a movement within us. The key is **observing**. The heart knows how to feel, but it must be accompanied by awareness.

Dimensions of Awakening:
HEART – The Chamber of Longing and Recognition

The heart does not think. It remembers. It doesn't solve—it feels. The heart's intelligence is ancient, and its ache is often the first whisper that something deeper calls.

- **Yearning**
  A hunger with no clear object. You ache for something you can't name. This is the soul tapping on the heart's inner walls: *"There is more. Come find it."*
- **Recognition**
  The déjà vu of the soul. You meet someone, hear a phrase, see a place—and suddenly, you remember. This is not new. It's anciently familiar.
- **Disillusionment**
  When the truth breaks your heart. What you trusted was false. It is painful—but it's pure. The cracking is how the light enters.
- **Soul Encounter**
  You meet a being who reflects your essence. Love may be there, but this isn't romance—it's awakening. A mirror that refuses to let you remain asleep.
- **Epiphany (Heart-centered)**
  Not a thought—but a feeling so resonant it teaches the mind. The moment you realize: *"I've been holding back my truth. And now it's time to open."*

Emotional Embodiment Practices

- **Inner child work**: Reconnecting with the younger self that never got to feel safely
- **Sacred grief rituals**: Creating containers to honor loss and mourning
- **Authentic expression**: Voice dialogue, crying, poetry, song
- **Heart coherence meditation**: Synchronizing breath, body, and emotion
- **Presence with emotion**: Letting feeling move through without labeling or suppressing

"There is a crack in everything. That's how the light gets in."
— Leonard Cohen

Heart's Invitation:
Let yourself be pierced by what matters.

Reflection

When we awaken emotionally, we return to the most ancient truth of all — That we are not machines. We are beings. That tears are sacred.

That joy is prayer. That love is not a goal it is our essence.

Emotional awakening brings the soul online through the portal of the heart. It does not remove pain — it allows pain to reveal us. And through that revelation, the soul begins to shine.

Intuitive Awakening
Subtle Knowing - Inner Guidance
Nonlinear Insight

"The intuitive mind is a sacred gift and the rational mind is a faithful servant. We have created a society that honors the servant and has forgotten the gift."— Bob Samples, The Metaphoric Mind (1976)

Part One frames intuition as the bridge between worlds, the whisper that bypasses logic. Part Two explores how this inner compass functions in practice — through sensitivity, gut knowing, and the quiet trust that guides us beyond intellect.

There is a kind of knowing that doesn't come from thought.
It doesn't arrive through reason, analysis, or logic.
It comes quietly — as a nudge, a pull, a whisper in the stillness.

This is intuition: the psyche's subtle guidance system. Intuitive awakening begins the moment we start listening — the moment we stop demanding proof, and start responding to the pulse. It is not about certainty. It is about trust.

"The only real valuable thing is intuition." — Albert Einstein

The Language Beneath Thought

Intuition does not speak in paragraphs. It speaks in resonance:

- A feeling in the belly

- A warmth in the chest
- A shiver up the spine

It's the "yes" before the mind can explain. The "no" that echoes through the body like a bell.

> *"Intuition is seeing with the soul."*
> *— Dean Koontz*

To awaken intuitively is to follow the breadcrumbs of inner guidance. To navigate not by map, but by magnet. It is not about knowing the entire path, only the next step that carries a deep, embodied yes.

The Reclamation of Inner Guidance

> *"Intuition is not a step backward from reason;*
> *it is a leap beyond it."— JaiViibes*

We are conditioned to trust proof, rules, experts, and systems. The inner voice is often silenced under layers of "should" and "must." Intuitive awakening is the reclamation of that voice — the remembering that your soul has been whispering all along.

It requires a subtle shift: from outsourcing truth to reclaiming it. From seeking authority outside, to listening within. From analyzing endlessly, to responding to resonance.

Signs of Intuitive Awakening

- Heightened sensitivity to people, spaces, or energy
- Sudden insights or inner knowing without rational basis
- Pulls toward certain places, paths, or practices
- Discomfort with purely logical or linear decision-making
- Increasing synchronicities or meaningful "coincidences"

These are not hallucinations. They are echoes of guidance surfacing — signals that your inner compass is switching back on.

The Shadow of Intuition

Unmoored from grounding, intuition can distort into fantasy. It can be mistaken for impulse, fear, or ego-driven desire. Trauma echoes may masquerade as inner guidance, leading us to repeat old patterns under the illusion of "knowing."

The intuitive path requires embodiment. Intuition must be tethered to body, tempered by heart, and aligned with soul. Otherwise, it becomes projection, escapism, or self-deception.

Trusting intuition does not guarantee perfection. But it ensures alignment. Even when the path bends unexpectedly, the act of listening deepens coherence with one's essence.

Dimensions of Awakening:
INTUITION - The Compass of the Unspoken

Intuition doesn't explain — it perceives. It lives in the liminal, in the pause before language, in the subtle yes or sudden no that arrives before reason.

- **Lucid Moment:** A flash of clarity, as if the veil lifts. Quick, but undeniable.
- **Download:** A phrase, image, or knowing that arrives whole, bypassing thought. It feels both foreign and deeply yours.
- **Somatic Signal:** A bodily cue — contraction, expansion, tingling — that reveals truth faster than thought.
- **Symbolic Encounter:** Dreams, synchronicities, or repeating images that orient you to meaning.
- **Integration:** Acting on intuition consistently, allowing it to reshape the nervous system into trust rather than doubt.

Practices to Strengthen Intuition

- **Stillness and solitude:** intuition cannot compete with noise
- **Freewriting:** bypassing the mind by letting the pen move freely
- **Body listening:** allowing sensation to inform decisions
- **Symbol work and dream journaling:** giving language to the unconscious
- **Play and spontaneity:** intuition thrives in openness, not rigidity

Each practice trains us to notice subtle cues, to give them space, and to act on them without over-analysis.

Intuitive awakening is not about escaping reason, but about expanding beyond it. It is learning to recognize the language beneath thought, to reclaim the compass of your own being, and to trust the whisper that has always been there

Intuition's Invitation:
Trust the truth that has no explanation.

Reflection

*Intuition is not an extra sense. It is the original sense.
The one we were all born with.
The one we were conditioned to ignore.*

*To awaken intuitively is to return to that original
connection — To live not just from what you know,
but from what your soul remembers.*

Soul Awakening
Presence - Essence - Divine Remembering

"You are not a human being having a spiritual experience. You are a spiritual being having a human experience."
— *Wayne Dyer*

Part One presents the soul as the eternal spark, the essence that remembers beyond time. Part Two turns toward the lived psychology of soul — the crises of meaning, the hunger for purpose, and the moments of presence that reorient us toward what is Real.

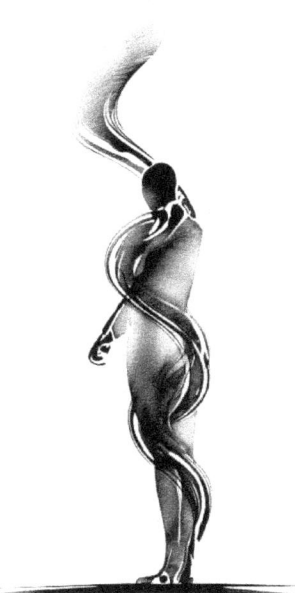

The soul does not awaken like the mind, body, or heart.
It does not unfold or burst open.
The soul remembers.
It always has. It always will.

But in a world obsessed with proof and appearances, the soul can go quiet — buried beneath identities, numbed by survival, shrouded in forgetting. Soul awakening is the moment of remembering what cannot be learned. It is not about discovering a new self, but uncovering the original self.

The Essence Beneath the Story

You are not your name. Not your job. Not your trauma. Not even your personality.

These are garments the soul wears — temporary masks for the eternal actor. The soul is the flame behind the eyes, the silence beneath the thought, the hum you feel in awe, grief, beauty, or stillness.

To awaken at the level of soul is not to become something greater — it is to shed what is not you, until only truth remains.

> *"The soul is like a wild animal — tough, resilient, and shy. It seeks silence, stillness, and is revealed slowly, not through force, but through invitation."* — Parker J. Palmer

The Great Unveiling

Soul awakening often comes after the other layers have been softened — after the body has released, the mind has questioned, the heart has wept, and intuition has whispered.

Suddenly, there is no more seeking. Only being.

It can arrive in meditation, in nature, in grief, or in laughter. In those moments, something ancient opens its eyes within you. You don't just feel alive — you remember that you *are* Life itself.

The soul awakens not because it was missing, but because we became still enough to hear it.

Signs of Soul Awakening

> *"The whisper you keep hearing isn't your imagination. It's your soul calling you home."— JaiViibes*

- A profound sense of being in the now or timelessness
- Detachment from old roles or identities
- Deep peace without external cause
- Spontaneous feelings of unity, reverence, or devotion
- A call to serve, create, or live from authenticity

These aren't goals to chase, but results of deep letting go.

The Shadow of Soul Awakening

Awakening at the soul level is not only blissful — it can be destabilizing. The soul dismantles illusions, and in that dismantling, shadows emerge.

- **Grief of Shedding**: Awakening brings loss — of false identities, long-held ambitions, or relationships no longer aligned. Even as it is liberating, it carries the grief of what must fall away.
- **Loneliness of Vision**: The more the soul comes online, the more dissonance you may feel with a culture built on ego and pretense. The awakened soul sees differently, and not everyone is ready to walk beside that vision.
- **Disorientation of Dissolution**: When roles, beliefs, and identities dissolve, a void can open. This is not failure, but liminality — the in-between where the old no longer fits and the new has not yet fully arrived.

- **Inflation**: Another shadow is spiritual pride — mistaking glimpses of soul for superiority. This can isolate further and distort the awakening process, pulling one away from humility.
- **Avoidance**: Sometimes awakening feels so vast it triggers retreat — a pulling back into numbness, denial, or distractions, because the soul's vastness feels overwhelming to the small self.

This is sacred disintegration — the cocoon softening before the wings emerge. The shadow is not a detour from awakening, but part of its alchemy. To face it with humility, patience, and compassion is to allow the soul to anchor more fully in our human life.

Dimensions of Awakening:
SOUL - The Flame Behind All Seeing

The soul is not a thing — it is a presence. It does not awaken — it awakens *you*. When it takes the lead, life itself becomes holy.

- **Spiritual Awakening:** The shift from living as the self to living from the soul. It may arrive through crisis, grace, or mystery.
- **Initiation:** Crossing a threshold where the old self dies and a new way of being begins.
- **Mystical Union (Soul-Realized):** Not just feeling oneness, but remembering you *are* the One. The soul takes the throne, and the ego bows.

- **Sacred Silence:** The holy hush beneath all noise. Not emptiness, but fullness without form. To rest here is to sit in the center of being.

Revelation (Soul-Seeded): A truth that transforms not just what you know, but who you are. The soul speaks, and your life reorders itself in service of that knowing.

Soul Practices & Invitations

- **Contemplative silence:** sitting beyond thought, beyond image, in simple being
- **Nature immersion:** allowing Earth to mirror soul in form
- **Devotional practice:** prayer, chanting, ritual, or acts of service
- **Creative expression:** art, song, writing, movement — the soul's exhale
- **Sacred ordinary:** letting daily life become temple, noticing the holy in what seems mundane

Each practice is less about effort, more about opening. They are invitations, not requirements.

Soul awakening is not the arrival of something new, but the unveiling of what has always been. It is the gentle yet seismic remembering that presence itself is your essence — and when the soul leads, life becomes devotion.

Soul's Invitation:
Come home.

Reflection

The soul is not separate from you. It is you.
Not the conditioned you, not the performative you

— but the infinite, luminous awareness that has
watched it all unfold.

To awaken the soul is not to become more.
It is to become real. This is the final return.
Not to a place. But to presence.

Closing Summary
Book One: Awakening

*Awakening does not end with light, it begins and continues with loss.
Not of the real, but of illusion. Not of the true self,
but of the story we mistook for self.
We have felt the veil lift, the ground shift, the false structures tremble
and fall. And in the quiet that follows, a deeper recognition arises:*

I am not who I thought I was.

*This is not clarity—it is rupture, a sacred disorientation.
The crumbling of inherited identities, unquestioned roles,
and conditioned beliefs. We have tasted freedom, but we are still
tangled in the threads of the self, unaware. A self shaped by survival,
by culture, by unconscious choice. A self that performed to belong, that
adapted to be safe, that was unaware of more than the mask.*

*As this false self begins to dissolve, we meet the real work of
awakening: To question. To observe. To map the contours of our
conditioning. To sit with the discomfort of dissociation,
disillusionment, and cognitive dissonance.*

*Awakening was the spark that lit a fire
of evolving awareness. Now begins the excavation.*

*As we continue, we turn inward—not to demolish the self,
but to uncover what shaped it, and to dismantle it.*

Book Two: The Self
*begins here. Not with answers,
but with honest inquiry.*

Appendix

A. Core Differentiation – Trinity vs Five-Fold

Framework	Focus	Function in Book 1	Relation
Trinity of Soul – Self – Creation	Cosmological	Explains *how existence itself* moves—Soul initiates, Self translates, Creation resonates.	The "big picture" circuit of reality.
Five-Fold Human	Psychological / Embodied	Explains *how the human being* experiences that circuit—Body, Mind, Heart, Intuition, Soul.	A study of the inner instrument within the larger circuit.

We use different combinations—like the trinity or the five-fold map—not to complicate things, but because each lens teaches us to see from another angle of the same whole.

B. Book 2 Evolution — the Prism Shift

Aspect	Book 1 Image	Book 2 Image	Core Shift
Self	Cocoon / Vehicle	**Prism**	From container to conductor of light
Soul	Seed germinating within	**Light beam** entering and illuminating	From latent spark to active radiance
Creation	The encompassing field	**Reflected spectrum** of expression	From backdrop to participatory resonance

In later volumes, this trinity widens. The self that first felt like a cocoon begins to act as a prism, letting the soul's light refract into color. What once felt separate—soul, self, and creation—starts to reveal itself as one field of living light.

Continue the Exploration

If something in this book has stirred questions, you are not alone. For many readers, the conversation does not end when the final page closes. It begins.

If you would like a steady place to continue the exploration, and guidance for integrating what may be unfolding, you are welcome to begin here.

https://www.jaiviibes.com/support

www.ingramcontent.com/pod-product-compliance
Lightning Source LLC
LaVergne TN
LVHW050024080526
838202LV00069B/6900